D1568975

31 Small Steps to Organize for Emergencies
(and Disasters)

a dhucks small steps book by
Shawndra Holmberg, CPO-CD®

Copyright © 2018 Shawndra Holmberg

All rights reserved. This book or any portion thereof may not be reproduced or used in any manner whatsoever without the express written permission of the author except for the use of brief quotations in a book review, blog or article, with attribution to author and book title.

Although the author and publisher have made every effort to ensure that the information in this book was correct at press time, the author and publisher do not assume and hereby disclaim any liability to any party for any loss, damage, or disruption caused by errors or omissions, whether such errors or omissions result from negligence, accident, or any other cause. This book is for informational purposes only. All decisions and actions taken in preparation for and responding to emergencies and disasters is the responsibility of the individual.

References are provided for informational purposes only. Readers should be aware that the websites listed in this book may change. The author may recommend certain products and services. The author has no financial relationship with these companies.

ISBN-10: 1984161695

ISBN-13: 978-1984161697

Cover art copyright © 2018 Shawndra Holmberg

books by
Shawndra Holmberg

31 Small Steps to Organize Your Life
31 Small Steps to Organize for Weight Loss
31 Small Steps to Organize Your Paper

Table of Contents

what did you say this book was about?

This book is not intended to be a survival guide if life as we know it crumbles. This book is for those who understand that emergencies and disasters can happen to individuals, families, communities, and geographical regions, and who want to be ready to handle them better. A winter storm can take out your electricity for days or even weeks. A hurricane may threaten your city and you have to shelter in place or choose to evacuate until it passes. A tornado carves a path of devastation and utilities are disrupted; you're fine but you have no electricity or water. There's a fire in your building and you have to evacuate with the basic necessities. A tree crashes down on your house and you have to find other accommodations until repairs are made. Or you're stuck in your car on the highway due to a major accident ahead.

You will be planning and preparing for large emergencies, which means you'll be better prepared for the smaller emergencies. If an emergency happens, your life will be affected, but you'll handle it better if you take these 31 Small Steps to Organize for Emergencies.

The widespread sharing of danger, loss, and deprivation produces an intimate, primarily group solidarity among the survivors, which overcomes social isolation, provides a channel for intimate communication and expression, and provides a major source of physical and emotional support and reassurance.

Charles E. Fritz

what's the best way to take these small steps?

Anything you can do needs to be done, so pick up the tool of your choice and get started.

Ben Linder

Well, that's kind of up to you. It's your book! But I think the best way to go about it is one step at a time, one chapter each day. Don't read them all in one sitting without taking action.

Could you pick a step at random and work on it? Certainly. There may be a reference to a previous step or even a future step, but most of the steps can be accomplished in whatever order you take them. You could even — if you're feeling contrary — start at the end and go backwards! It doesn't matter. The whole point of taking these 31 Small Steps is to keep things simple and to minimize the overwhelm. Whatever approach you choose, pick one idea each day and take that small step!

If there is a step that doesn't make sense to you, or it isn't in the order you want, or you just don't feel like doing it — mark it for review later and move on. Don't stop. Don't toss out the rest of the steps. Don't struggle. Mark it and move on. Keep going.

Pick ONE action to take and move forward to the next Step.

Each of these 31 Small Steps has one or more key actions to choose from to become better prepared. There are usually additional actions you *could* take, but I don't want you to get bogged down. At the end of each Step, I've listed the key actions to choose from under **Pick ONE action to take today**. Focus on that one action.

There will be additional actions you can take to increase your preparedness under **Possible Next Actions.** Sure, go ahead and read the list to see if there are things you can easily do now, prefer to do instead, or might do the next time through. But don't get bogged down, stuck, overwhelmed or, worse, stopped by all the things you could do.

Think of preparedness as an ongoing, never perfect, process. There is no endpoint you can reach that says you're prepared. It's the path of learning, practicing, adding, and refining that helps you become better able to respond effectively during an emergency or disaster.

After each step, I've added a section for your notes, scribbles, or doodles. You also have a wide margin for note taking. Highlight sections, quotes, or ideas you want to check out again. If the thought of writing in the book is horrifying, think of this as a workbook. You're supposed to write your answers and ideas in it. If, after writing notes in each section, you find you must have a book free of marks, send your marked-up book to me at Shawndra Holmberg, 140 Shockey Lane, Building F, PMB# 110, Butler, PA 16001, and I'll send you a new book. Email me at simplify@dhucks.com to let me know it's coming and to make sure the mailing address is still current.

Throughout this book you will be making lists, forming plans, and gathering documents. These will go into your Personal Information Center (PIC) Notebook. I'll cover the details in Step #11, but you'll need to collect them as you go. I recommend using 3-ring binder that is at least 2" wide, but you can use any folder or notebook you choose. Start with what you have on hand and change when you're ready.

disaster, emergency, or just the unexpected

Some people don't like change, but you need to embrace change if the alternative is disaster.

Elon Musk

When you think of emergencies and disasters, you may picture hurricanes, tornadoes, floods, or blizzards. This book is intended to help you be better prepared for those types of emergencies and disasters.

But a disaster does not have to affect your whole community. A disaster is **anything that overwhelms your resources**. Sometimes things can happen just to you or your family. It can be as routine as your car needing repair. It could be a fire that destroys your home or a water heater that floods your basement. These steps will also prepare you for those more immediate and personal emergencies.

The agencies in your community that are responsible for preparing for, preventing, responding to, and recovering from emergencies may be identified as emergency management, emergency services, civil defense, civil preparedness, or disaster services. I will be using the term emergency management.

Search online or call your local government to find what department is responsible for emergency management for your community and get to know them or at least what they do.

this is not a survival guide

As I previously mentioned, this book is not intended to be a survival guide if life as we know it crumbles. This book is focused on planning and preparing to respond to events where civil society continues, neighbors help neighbors, each individual actively participates in their own response, and organizations help us get on our feet again.

While you're preparing, consider how you'll respond in various situations (play the 'what-if' game). This is part of the planning process. As you think about what you'd do in the emergency or disaster also consider what you can do to prevent your situation from getting worse. I know you can't prevent a hurricane or a winter storm, but could you take action to prevent your roof being ripped off by adding hurricane clips? Could you get a licensed electrician in to install GFCI (ground fault circuit interrupter) outlets and purchase a new space heater so that a house fire is less likely? What can you do to prevent the disaster or minimize the consequences?

I believe luck is preparation meeting opportunity. If you hadn't been prepared when the opportunity came along, you wouldn't have been lucky.

Oprah Winfrey

what emergencies and disasters will you prepare for?

...it is important to be prepared for the unthinkable. Supplies and a plan will significantly reduce panic and chaos in the event of an emergency.

Sen. Mike Crapo
Idaho, 1993-1999

To be prepared for emergencies and disasters, you need to know what hazards you might face, plan for the actions you'll take, and look at mitigating (removing or reducing) those hazards.

Let's start by identifying the hazards you're likely to face in your community. Check off all hazards in the list below that have happened in your community or state in the last 3 years. If you're not sure, go to www.fema.gov/disasters to see what declared disasters have happened in your state or territory. You could also check off the ones you've personally experienced. If there's one hazard you're particularly concerned about, check that one as well.

After you've checked the hazards, I'll have you narrow your focus further. No need to get overwhelmed by planning for all the hazards. You will be better prepared for any of them once you've prepared for one.

If you prefer not to write in your book, download the list at www.dhucks.com/resources-31-smallsteps-emergencies. Print a copy to refer to as you work through each step.

The list is not in order of priority but rather alphabetical. I've only listed common hazards in this section. For a full list of hazards go to Appendix P — Hazards & Mitigation.

HAZARDS (check the hazards you're likely to face)

- ❑ Active Shooter (if you have children in school, does the school have an Active Shooter plan?)

- ❑ Dam/Levee Failures

- ❑ Earthquakes

- ❑ Extreme Heat (heat wave)

- ❑ Floods

- ❑ Gremlins

- ❑ Hazardous Materials Incidents (do you live near a railway or a road with truck traffic?)

- ❑ House Fires

- ❑ Household Chemical Emergencies

- ❑ Hurricanes

- ❑ Nuclear Blast

- ❑ Nuclear Power Plants

- ❑ Pandemic

- ❑ Power Outages

- ❑ Snowstorms and Extreme Cold

- ❑ Thunderstorms and Lightning

- ❑ Tornadoes

- ❑ Tribbles

- ❑ Tsunamis

- ❑ Volcanoes and Lava Flow (volcanic eruption)

- ❑ Wildfires

- ❑ Zombies

Now that you've checked off all the threats and hazards you or your community have faced, choose the three that you're most concerned about and willing to plan and prepare for. Go ahead and highlight or mark those three. Once you've identified the three, which one is more important for you to prepare for? The next most important?

What are your top three hazards again?

#1: _____

#2: _____

#3: _____

Today's Date: _____

Your objective, as you go through the next 31 Small Steps, is to prepare for your #1 hazard. You'll be better prepared for the remaining hazards, but you need to start somewhere. Keep your focus on the #1 hazard and move through the steps. Once you're better prepared for the #1 hazard, you can go back and review the steps and plan and prepare for the #2 hazard, etc.

These 31 Steps and focusing on one hazard are intended to keep you moving forward, prevent you from becoming overwhelmed, and ensure you are better prepared at each step. Focus on what you have accomplished and what is in your power to prevent and prepare for.

Take the first step. Then take the next. And then the next.

Keep moving forward.

If, after reading through the list of hazards you're preparing for, you feel overwhelmed, too scared to move forward and take action — BREATHE. Then take the first step — Step #1.

If there is one particular hazard you want to skip, because just the idea of it stresses you, that's okay for now. Focus on preparing to deal with a hazard that has less emotional baggage attached. Take action to become better prepared through these 31 Small Steps. After you've gone through all the Steps once, come back and work on preparations for that hazard you skipped earlier. Ignoring the hazard won't make it go away or become less real, but facing it after you've prepared for another hazard will make it more manageable.

If you want to get prepared but find yourself making excuses to do it later, consider preparing with a buddy or hiring a professional organizer to help. You can search for an organizer near you through either NAPO (National Association of Productivity and Organizing Professionals, www.napo.net) or ICD (Institute for Challenging Disorganization, challengingdisorganization.org). You can also work with an organizer who works over the phone or video (via Skype, Facetime etc.) with clients like I do. You can contact me through Dhucks.com.

If you have feelings of dread or fear that continually stop you from taking these 31 Small Steps, talk to someone you trust for the additional emotional, physical, and mental support you may need.

use a timer

Take these 31 Small Steps one at a time. Break your work on each step into shorter, more manageable chunks of time such as 10 or 15 minutes or a half hour — whatever is doable for you. Make it short enough so you can stay focused, but long enough so you can get things done. By using a timer, you'll be able to tell yourself you'll be setting limits on the total time you spend planning and preparing.

It's not about spending your life building up your emergency supplies. It's about setting aside time to take action so if an emergency or disaster does affect you, you'll be better prepared.

For a timer, you can use the clock on your phone, an app, or a kitchen timer. I recommend Time Timer® for clients as it provides a visual cue of time passing with its red wheel counting down. The Time Timer® can be purchased as an app (phone, tablet, or computer) or a physical timer.

Set your timer for 15 minutes, 20 minutes, or 30 minutes. The goal is to break down the time you've set aside to get prepared into smaller chunks of time. After 15 minutes (or your chosen chunk of time) the timer goes off to remind you to get back on task if you've gotten distracted, to take a break if you're feeling tired, to finish up for the day, or to encourage you to take on another 15 minutes because you've got the energy to continue.

In working with clients, I have found that setting a timer gives them permission to quit working on their task after fifteen minutes or an hour and fifteen minutes. They stop dreading the process, the preparation, and the maintenance because it no longer has to take their whole day.

Don't be fooled by the calendar. There are only as many days in the year as you can make use of.

Charles Richards

The goal is not to spend your life preparing, but to take time to prepare to handle the emergencies in your life.

ready to take that first step?

The best time to plant a tree is twenty years ago. The second best time is now.

Proverb

It won't bite. Dhucks don't have teeth!

Save Your Ones ($)

Yes, saving your $1s is a small step, but there's another important reason for having small bills on hand rather than $20s or even $10s. During a community-wide emergency, there may be individuals selling supplies. If they're selling a six-pack of bottled water for $15 and all you have is a $20, they may tell you they don't have change. Though price gouging isn't right, especially during an emergency, it does happen. If you really need the supplies and the gouger is the only source around, you might be willing to pay $15 and hand over the other $5. However, if you have one-dollar bills, you pay only what you must to get what you need.

Every accomplishment starts with the decision to try.

Gail Devers

I don't want you to get the idea that everyone will be out to take advantage of you in a disaster or emergency. In my experience, a community comes together to help and support each other and it's amazing how kind and giving people can be. But I also want you to be prepared to work around those individuals who aren't so civic-minded.

You don't have to set aside this cash all at once. Take your time and add your $1s to your stash each evening or weekend. If $200 is easy, increase your goal to $250 or $500 and add in $5s and $10s. Build up your emergency cash fund one bill at a time.

Collect your $1s each week and build up your cash stash over time.

WHERE TO STORE YOUR EMERGENCY CASH?

A safe place, of course. A place you'll remember and a place you can easily access if you need to grab and go. Place it in your emergency kit (which you'll be building over the next 30 small steps). Place it in your PIC (Personal Information Center), Step #11. Or decide on another location that works best for you.

In Step #31, you will establish an annual review or "check-by" date. Plan to exchange or rotate 25% of your cash for new bills each year. The bills won't expire of course, but they do start to smell musty after a while.

This emergency cash fund is not intended for you to use as a "I ran out of money and I need to buy groceries" fund but as a source for cash if you can't get to your bank accounts. During a disaster, your bank may not be open for business, and if the power is out, the ATMs won't work.

Your cash stash needs to be secure but also easy for *you* to grab.

Remember, your stash needs to be easy to access (and secure) as you may only have moments to grab what you can before evacuating your house.

SUMMARY

Pick ONE action to take today:

- ❑ Start saving your one-dollar bills until you collect $200

- ❑ Continue to save one-dollar bills until you reach your chosen limit

Possible Next Actions:

- ❑ Build up a savings fund for emergencies such as car repairs or a job loss. Your goal may be 3-6 months of expenses, but you can start small.

   This fund should be in an account separate from your normal everyday accounts so you don't dip into the reserve. Set your guidelines for use. You could decide that it's for the emergency repair on the car, home maintenance and preparedness, or a bigger emergency.

- ❑ Save 1% of your paycheck, then 5%, and build up to 10%. As most financial planners will tell you — pay yourself first when it comes to savings.

Add Notes Here ↘

ONE action today

- ❑ Start saving your one-dollar bills until you collect $200

- ❑ Continue to save one-dollar bills until you reach your chosen limit of _____

2 Fill Up Your Gas Tank at Half-empty

An ounce of prevention is worth a pound of cure.

Benjamin Franklin

Build a habit of filling up your car before it gets below half a tank.

As the saying goes "your car runs just as well on the top half of the tank as it does on the bottom half." Fill up your vehicle BEFORE it gets below half a tank. Make this a habit now so when the next big storm is expected to hit, you won't be wasting time in long gas lines with everyone else.

If you're not already doing this, it may take some mental effort to change your behavior. You may plan to fill up when the tank gets to a half, but you may think "I'll do it tomorrow" and tomorrow comes and goes with no stop at the gas station. If that's the case you could:

- Set one day a week when you make it a part of your routine. Decide whether you'll fill up every Monday on your way home from work, or Wednesday before you go shopping, or every Saturday on your way to the park. Build in the habit of filling up weekly if it helps keep your tank filled. If you fill up more often, set two days a week as routine stops at the gas station.

- Link filling up your gas tank with an activity. Grocery shopping or your weekly meeting can trigger a reminder to make a stop at the gas station too. Even if you're only down a quarter of a tank, fill up anyway. Keeping your tank full is a small step in becoming better prepared.

- If your car is routinely filled but other family members forget to fill theirs, consider offering to remind them to fill up when you fill up.

If you fill up later rather than sooner because you think it takes too long, time how long it takes to drive to your gas station, pull in, fill up, and head out. My guess is that it will take you a lot less time than you believe.

If you have time, check your tire pressure too. Maintaining your car in the best shape you can will improve your ability to respond and recover to an emergency or disaster.

SUMMARY

Pick ONE action to take today:

❑   Build the habit of filling your gas tank at half-full

Possible Next Actions:

❑   Add checking your tire pressure

❑   Remind friends and family to fill their gas tanks at half-full

Add Notes Here ⬂

ONE action today

❑   Build the habit of filling your gas tank at half-

Lines of Communication

Communication leads to community, that is, to understanding, intimacy and mutual valuing.

Rollo May

Keeping your lines of communication open and powered up during an emergency or disaster is important. The technology we use to do that has changed over the years. You need to be aware of how that change affects your ability to communicate in an emergency. Are you one of the 91+% of adults in the United States who owns a cell phone[1]? Are you one of the 49% (and dwindling) who choose to have a landline phone?[2]

Here are the key points you need to know:

51% of the U.S. population have chosen to give up their standard landline phone.

1. Standard landlines provide power for the phone even when the power goes out, but you must have a **corded** phone.

2. Keep your cell phones charged and get a portable power charger to recharge. Make it a habit to recharge your cell phones each night.

91% of U.S. adults own a cell phone.[2]

3. To conserve battery life, close all apps and turn off Wi-Fi and Bluetooth capability during an emergency. Don't turn off the phone as turning the phone off and on drains more energy.

4. Stay off the phone unless it's an emergency. Keep the phone lines open for emergency responders and personnel. Call 911 if you need emergency help.

5. If you don't have coverage (zero bars) call 911 anyway. There just might be enough bandwidth to get through. If the 'no coverage' is because you're in an area covered by another network, 911 calls are required to be connected regardless of your service provider.

6. Text rather than call family and friends. Your texts have a better chance of getting through during a

disaster/emergency than your calls do because they use less bandwidth. Refer back to #4 – stay off the phone.

7. Consider purchasing a pre-paid cell phone from a different service provider to broaden your coverage during an emergency.

PHONE SERVICE DURING AN EMERGENCY

Phone service during an emergency depends on what type of phone you have (cell, VoIP, standard landline), who's affected by the emergency (you or your service provider), and the extent of the emergency or disaster.

<u>Cellular</u>

If the power is out in your neighborhood, you may still have cell phone service if the service provider is not affected. If your service provider lost power and their backup generator isn't available or capable of handling the load, then you probably won't have phone coverage. In the 12 years I lived in Hawai'i, I went through numerous storms, power outages, and other natural disasters, but there was only one time that cell phone service wasn't available. It's likely that a simple power outage in your neighborhood will not affect your cell phone coverage.

However, if the disaster or emergency is wide spread, your calls may not go through. Either your mobile carrier may be affected or the vast number of calls being made is congesting the networks. This is where texting comes in handy. If your call won't go through, try texting. The lower bandwidth requirement of texts might allow it to slip through. If your text doesn't go through, it may be saved and transmitted later when capacity is available.

Text rather than call family and friends during a disaster.

During an emergency, most of us would prefer that our emergency responders be able to communicate. That's why the U.S. Department of Homeland Security has set up and manages the Wireless Priority Service (WPS). If you want to learn more about WPS go to www.dhs.gov/wireless-priority-service-wps.

If you need to call 911 from your cell phone, make the call regardless of what coverage your phone shows. Your 911 call may

Dial 911 even when it looks like you don't have coverage or enough

go through regardless of your provider. If the bandwidth is too low for a routine call (showing zero bars) you may still have enough for an emergency call.

The Federal Communications Commission (FCC) established basic 911 rules which requires all wireless service providers to transmit 911 calls regardless of whether the caller is a subscriber or not. The FCC also established enhanced 911 rules which provide your phone number and location to emergency responders.

VoIP

VoIP or Voice over Internet Protocol phones are becoming more common in homes as many Internet providers offer the option. If you have a VoIP phone, find and read the information the company gave you that explains the 911 limitations or enhancements and any emergency or disaster guidelines.

If your power goes out, your phone is out. If your internet is down, your phone is down. However, your provider may have an app available for your smartphone that won't be affected by the power outage that is affecting your home. If you're not already familiar with your provider's app, get it and learn how to use it BEFORE an emergency. Of course, you could have power, but if your provider doesn't, the network is down and you're still without a phone.

Give 911 your **physical location first** even before your name.

If you're disconnected, **call back**.

When calling 911 from your VoIP phone give your physical location first even before your name. Because your VoIP number is not necessarily transmitted to the emergency call center, if you're disconnected, call back.

The FCC has established some 911 rules for your VoIP provider but there may be limitations. Check the material you were given when you signed up. Also, make sure your physical address is current — not your billing address, but your physical address.

Standard Landline

Fewer than 50% of the US population currently have a standard landline (aka wireline) phone. If you're one of them, excellent! Purchase a corded phone (if you don't already have one) that does not require you to plug it in to a power outlet. No wireless handsets, no voice messaging, and no Caller ID.

The common style of corded phone that doesn't require external power is a Trimline phone. Other terms may be slim-line or princess. A Trimline phone is the most common and inexpensive style of corded phone.

Trimline corded phone

During a power outage you will have phone service (assuming the phone lines aren't down in the emergency) because the Trimline corded phone draws the small amount of power it needs from the phone line itself. You may routinely use a cordless phone/handset that requires you to put it back in the cradle for recharging. This set will not work if the power is out. But if you have that Trimline corded phone stashed next to your emergency light (flashlight or battery-operated lantern, Step #4) then you can plug it in when you need to and have communication capability.

Whether you have a cell, VoIP, or landline phone — STAY OFF THE PHONE unless you need to call for help. This allows the phone lines to be used by emergency first responders and those who need their help.

STAY OFF THE PHONE unless you need to call for help.

BUILD YOUR POWER PLAN

Each of the following sections includes suggested items to have or purchase. You do not have to get all of them at once. Start with adding one item to build your Power Plan now and add more as you can. Remember, the idea is to become better prepared, not best prepared or nothing.

Cellular

If you don't already have a car charger for your phone, get one. If all other power sources are out, you can use your car to charge your phone.

One item you might want for everyday use and for emergencies is a USB adapter that is charge only or data blocking. It is also referred to as a USB condom. Take one with you when you travel so no one can steal your data while you're charging your electronics in the airport or other public accessed charging station.

Purchase a portable charger (aka external battery, power bank, battery pack, power pack, or external battery) for your cell phone.

You could also purchase a hand-crank charger for your phone, but believe me, you'll get tired of cranking long before your phone is fully charged. As for a solar-powered charger, save your money at this time and focus on the previous options first.

Conserve power by:

❑ closing all apps;

❑ shutting off the Wi-Fi;

❑ lowering the brightness of the screen

❑ turning off the Bluetooth option; and

❑ turning off the Cellular Data access for all apps you don't need.

Closing all open apps will help, but some apps are still using data, Wi-Fi, and power even when closed. Shutting off the Wi-Fi will help, but some apps will continue to use your Cellular Data. You will need to turn off data access for individual apps.

Take 15 minutes now to look at the buttons and options on your phone. You may just find something you didn't know about that will come in handy today or during the next emergency.

Closing the open apps will depend on your phone. Search for "force close" on your phone or computer. But in general, Android users will need to go to settings and choose the Applications>Application Manager>Running and stop each application individually. Users of the iPhone8 or earlier will double click the Home button and then swipe up on each open app. For iPhone X users, you'll swipe up and pause; then touch and hold an app; then swipe up to close it.

Wi-Fi, Bluetooth, and Cellular Data options are found in the settings section of your phone. You could also turn the airplane mode on to limit power consumption, but do this if your plan is to make outgoing calls <u>only</u> and you don't need to receive incoming calls.

VoIP

Installing a backup power supply or an uninterruptible power supply (UPS) system can power your VoIP phone as long as the internet is up and all your equipment is on the UPS system — this includes your phone, your router and any other devices required for internet access. But if the internet is down, a backup power supply will not help you communicate.

Standard Landline

Buy a basic, no frills Trimline corded phone and sit back and relax. Any electricity needed for a phone call is provided on the telephone wires.

Buy a corded phone for your standard landline to use during a power outage.

Though I've covered a lot of information in this step and suggested many tools and supplies you might need, remember to make this step, Step #3 (Lines of Communication), doable today. Below is a list of possible items to add to your emergency supplies. Look over the list and **add ONE item** you don't already have. I've placed them in the order of importance, so start at the top and work your way down over time.

SUMMARY

Reduce power usage on your smartphone:

- Close all apps
- Turn off Wi-Fi
- Turn of apps accessing GPS location
- Lower brightness of screen
- Don't run down your car battery while using or charging your phone. Turn the engine on.

Pick ONE action to take today:

❑ Get a car charger for your cell phone — keep it in the car.

❑ Buy a Trimline corded phone if you have a landline — place it near your emergency lighting (Step #4) or near the phone outlet.

❑ Get a portable charger that can be recharged via a regular outlet or car charger. Add it to your Grab & Go checklist in Step #10.

Possible Next Actions:

❑ Buy a data blocking USB adaptor aka USB condom — add one to your emergency kit, travel kit, purse, briefcase, and more.

❑ Get an Uninterruptible Power Supply (UPS) for your VoIP system.

Resources:

- Who gets priority access: www.dhs.gov/wireless-priority-service-wps

Add Notes Here ⬊

ONE action today

❑ Car charger

❑ Trimline corded phone

❑ Portable power charger

Light

When the power goes out during a winter blizzard or a summer heat wave, you'll want to have light. Place a lantern, flashlight or other lighting option in an easy to reach spot so that you can get to it when the lights go out. There are more options than just the handheld flashlights of yesteryear.

There are flashlight apps available for your smartphone. But before you download an app, check to see if your phone has a built-in flashlight. It's on the Control Center screen of the iPhone and in Android it's on the Quick Access Panel (if you have a camera with a flash). Note on security of flashlight apps: your flashlight app will need to access your camera, but there's no reason for it to access your GPS or your contacts. Take time to review permissions and settings before download.

Your flashlight app is not intended to be your primary emergency light source. Using it drains your phone's battery. Using the flashlight on your phone is an excellent first light as you make your way to your emergency lantern or flashlight.

You can find small flashlights that can hang on your keychain. There are large, sturdy flashlights that can be used as a self-defense weapon or club if necessary. With the advent of LED bulbs there are flat flashlights that have magnets to hang on the nearest metal cabinet or pole.

You can purchase a head lamp. These come in handy if you want your hands free to clear debris, grill when the power is out (yes, we've done that), or anything else you need to have both hands available to do.

There are lanterns that run off batteries, are solar-powered, are rechargeable from your car or outlet, or a mix of power supply options. A lantern is a good option to include in your emergency supplies because it will stand (or hang) on its own and provide general lighting for your area. Most, if not all, battery/solar

Success depends on previous preparation.

Confucius

Your phone's flashlight app may be your initial emergency lighting source. Add a flashlight or lantern for long-term use.

powered lanterns have LED bulbs. When buying a lantern, you'll need to decide on the brightness you need as well as the battery life you want. The brighter (or more lumens) you want, the shorter the battery life. Look for a lantern with two light settings (high and low) so you can choose what you need in the moment.

Will the flashlight/lantern be only for emergencies or will it do double duty for camping, outdoor lighting options, or crawl-under-the-house-to-fix-a-leak lighting? Determine what you need your emergency light source to do besides being there for you in a disaster. Consider multiple flashlights and a lantern. Add a flashlight to your emergency kit. Carry a flashlight in your car. Take a small one with you traveling and keep it by your bed in case you need to leave the hotel room and the power's out.

Your flashlights and lanterns are only as good as the power supply. Whether you use the flashlight throughout the year or not, change out the batteries or recharge annually. Consider using the 2nd Sunday in March (Daylight Saving Time begins) or the 1st Sunday in November (Daylight Saving Time ends) as a reminder since it is Check Your Batteries Day. If you use your gear routinely for camping, picnics, or just backyard enjoyment, have extra batteries in stock or re-charge often. My personal experience with the hand cranked flashlights and the "shake" charged flashlights has led me to stick with battery-operated light sources. It's just not worth the effort or money and you'll get tired of cranking long before you've got enough light.

Keep candles for mood lighting, not emergency lighting. You don't want to add to the emergency by setting fire to your home because you knocked over a candle or it was set too close to a flammable object. And never leave a candle unattended.

One last thing to do when you choose your flashlight or lantern for your emergency supplies: Try it out! Play with it. Find out what all the buttons do. Even read the manual. 😳

Learn what your lighting source can and cannot do BEFORE an emergency. When you change out the batteries or re-charge, take a few minutes to remind yourself what that knob does, or what that thingy is on the back.

Change your clocks. Change your batteries!

Find out what your lighting source can do before the emergency.

SUMMARY

Pick ONE action to take today:

❑ Add a flashlight or lantern to your emergency kit

Possible Next Actions:

❑ Get a flashlight or lantern for home, car, or travel

❑ Try out your lantern or flashlight.

Add Notes Here ⬊

ONE action today

❑ Add a flashlight or lantern to the emergency kit

First Aid Kit

Hope for the best, prepare for the worst.

Chris Bradford

A first aid kit in every car.

First Aid, as the name implies, is the aid that is first given in case of a cut, puncture, sprain (even break), bite, sting or rash. It is given by you, your family, your friends, and even strangers who have no medical training.

You probably have a first aid kit at home or at least you have the supplies and bandages that make up one. But do you have one in your car? In this step, you'll put a first aid kit in your car. Yes, you will need a first aid kit in your emergency kit, but start with a basic first aid kit in every car. You use your car almost every day so be prepared daily. You can build your own kit or start with a store-bought kit.

If you purchase your first aid kits, please look through them and add any additional items you think you might need. The five basic situations you're stocking your first aid kit for are: bleeding, sprains/breaks, bites/stings/rashes, weather extremes, and physical collapse.

Here are a few things to include or ensure it's in your car's kit:

- ❑ Adhesive bandages, large strips

- ❑ Bandages, thumb or finger

- ❑ Bandages, 2-3 large square

- ❑ Bandage or adhesive tape

- ❑ Elastic bandage wrap, self-cling bandage wrap

- ❑ Antibiotic salve or spray

- ❑ Hydrocortisone or anti-itch cream

- ❑ Sunburn relief spray, gel or lotion

- ❑ Pain reliever

- ❑ Tweezers (blunt tipped, needle-nose pliers, or hemostats — to remove splinters and foreign object)

- ❑ Scissors

- ❑ Medicine dropper or needleless syringe

- ❑ Safety pins, a mix of medium and large

- ❑ Sterile saline wash (for cleaning wounds)

- ❑ Eye wash solution

- ❑ Hand sanitizer

- ❑ Moistened towelettes

- ❑ Non-latex disposable gloves

- ❑ Cold packs

- ❑ Heat packs

- ❑ Poison Control Center number: 1-800-222-1222 and online at www.PoisonHelp.org.

> Add the Poison Control Center number to your phone contacts.
>
> 1-800-222-1222
> www.PoisonHelp.org

Poison centers offer free, confidential, expert medical advice 24 hours a day, seven days a week through the Poison Help line at 1-800-222-1222 and online at www.PoisonHelp.org.

Once you've got a well-stocked first aid kit in *your* car, put a kit in every car and vehicle in your household. Once you've got a kit in every car, build or upgrade your home's first aid kit.

For the home kit, include all the previously listed items and add these:

- ❑ Anti-diarrhea medication

- ❑ Laxatives

❑ Syrup of ipecac to cause vomiting IF ADVISED by the Poison Control Center

❑ Activated charcoal to stop vomiting IF ADVISED by the Poison Control Center

❑ Bubble wrap for splinting

Add any additional items to your first aid kits (car or home) that your family uses or may need. Some non-standard options I always have in my home first aid kit and routinely add when camping or traveling are:

❑ Arnica Montana salve and pills for bruises and muscle soreness.

❑ Ichthammol — drawing salve — for splinters, bug bites, etc. — STINKS and is messy but amazing!

Once you have fully-stocked first aid kits in your home and car, get one for your emergency kit. Include a first aid book. Most of the first aid kits you can purchase come with a short first aid guide. If not, find a guide and add it. Get a first aid app on your phone.

Go low-tech — get a paperback or hardback copy of a first aid book.

In addition, purchase a first aid book for your emergency kit. An ebook is great to have but consider getting a print copy of the first aid book in case the power is out. I also suggest a first aid kit and book for your pets in Step #9.

You'll schedule an annual review of your emergency supplies in Step #31 (Annual Check and Refresh). Be sure to include your first aid kits in the review. Change out any supplies that don't look or smell like they should. Your over-the-counter (OTC) medical supplies have an expiration date, which guarantees the product retains its strength and quality if stored properly. The temperature extremes in a car are not proper storage temperatures and can degrade your first aid supplies. For more on expiration dates go to Step #7 (Build a Kit — Medications).

SUMMARY

Pick ONE action to take today:

- ❏ Buy or build a first aid kit for your car

- ❏ Buy or build a first aid kit for the other cars

Possible Next Actions:

- ❏ Buy or build a first aid kit for your home

- ❏ Buy or build a first aid kit for your emergency kit

- ❏ Purchase a first aid book in print.

- ❏ Take a First Aid or CPR/AED training class. Providing first aid is not intended to replace medical treatment if the situation warrants it, but rather to provide immediate help. Check out your local Red Cross at www.redcross.org/about-us/our-work/training-education.

Resources:

- • Poison Control Center: www.PoisonHelp.org

- • First Aid and CPR training: www.redcross.org/about-us/our-work/training-education

Add Notes Here ↘

ONE action today

- ❏ Get a first aid kit for your car

- ❏ Put a first aid kit

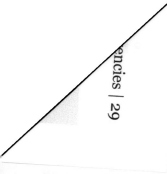

6 Build an Emergency Kit — Get a Bag

If you're having trouble starting something, the first step is too big.

Mary Solanto

Build an emergency kit that provides three days' worth of necessities and basic supplies. This kit is intended to be easily portable so you can take it with you if you have to evacuate quickly, which is why it's also been called a go-kit. The three days of supplies is intended to help you survive the first 72 hours of a disaster while local, state, and federal resources begin the recovery process, which is why it's also been called a 72-hour kit. This kit will also serve as the core of the emergency supplies you'll be gathering to stay put and shelter in place for longer than three days.

The focus of today's step is to **start** your emergency kit by getting a bag or box that will be easy to carry (remember the *go* part) and can hold the basics you'll need if you have to leave home in a hurry. A complete checklist of items to include in your emergency kit is in Appendix A — Emergency Kit Supply List. But for now — get a bag. You'll build the kit over time.

Find a bag or box to begin collecting the items you'll need. The best container would be a wheeled backpack. Ultimate mobility. You can wheel it to your car over smooth ground. Or throw it on your back and you still have your arms free to grab the next box or bag filled with emergency supplies. The next best container is one you already have.

Choose a bag, suitcase or container that can hold your supplies and GO with you if you have to evacuate.

Look around your home and find a duffel bag, a suitcase, or a plastic container that is small enough to carry but large enough to hold some basics. An overnight or a carry-on bag is about the right size to start. If you go with a plastic container, keep it small enough for you to carry. A water tight container with locking lid is preferred, but start with what you have on hand. As you continue to prepare, evaluate your emergency kit bag to see if you need to exchange it for something bigger, smaller, or more transportable.

If you're preparing for a family, start by getting one container for the family emergency kit, then add individual emergency kits as needed.

In Step #1, you started collecting one-dollar bills. Add your cash stash to your emergency kit or at least add a reminder to grab it.

Add any phone supplies from Step #3 (phones) and a flashlight from Step #4 (light) which you may have collected or purchased.

In Steps #7 and #8 you'll add an emergency supply of medicine and clothes to your emergency kit. As you proceed through the rest of the 31 Small Steps, add items to your emergency kit.

Add to your emergency kit as you take each of the next Small Steps.

Remember, make sure your kit remains easily portable even if you have to use a bigger bag or get another box. The emergency kit will be the first thing you grab so keep the priority items in there.

ONE action today

❏ Get a container for your emergency kit supplies

SUMMARY

Pick ONE action to take today:

❏ Find, get or buy one container for you or for your family to hold your emergency supplies.

Possible Next Actions:

❏ Build an individual kit for each family member.

❏ Build a kit to keep in your car; keep in mind temperature extremes that can affect some of the items you'll be adding to your emergency kit.

❏ Build a kit for every car in the family.

❏ Build a kit to keep at work.

Remember, the idea is to become better prepared, not do it all at one time (unless you have the time and money to do it all at once).

Resources:

• Appendix A — Emergency Kit Supply List

Add Notes Here ↘

Build an Emergency Kit — Add Medications

Do you have enough medicine in case of emergency? The more critical your medicine is to keeping you healthy and alive, the more important it is to have some in your emergency kit or at least to have more than two or three pills left before you refill your prescription.

Though most insurances policies still will not give you more than a 30-day supply when you fill your prescription at your local pharmacy, check to see if you can get a larger supply via your insurance's mail-order option. Many insurances offer a 90-day supply through mail order. If you choose to refill your prescription automatically, that might give you another 2 or 3 weeks. You can also change the shipping address easily if you need to evacuate your home.

For those over-the-counter (OTC) medicines you use (whether frequently or only when you need it, such as for colds, flu, or allergies), I recommend buying an extra bottle and keeping it in your emergency kit. You can then rotate your supplies by purchasing a new bottle or tube when you run low, placing the new OTC in your emergency kit and using the older medicine as your everyday supply. You can also do this with your prescription medicine if you have more than a 30-day supply.

Build this habit of restocking or exchanging your meds by setting a monthly reminder in your calendar or an alarm on your phone.

Do not keep your medicine, prescribed or OTC, in an emergency kit if it will be left in the car or another location that may experience temperature extremes. You could instead stash your emergency kit meds in a toiletry or travel bag that you store in the house. This will make it easy to grab (and update). Wherever you keep your emergency kit meds, ensure that the meds are secure and placed out of the reach of pets and children.

Luck is what happens when preparation meets opportunity.

Darrel Royal

The more important the medicine is to keeping you healthy and alive, the more important it is to have it in your emergency kit.

Having all your emergency medicines in a travel bag will simplify the exchange and updating of the supplies.

If you choose not to make a medicine kit or can't right now, don't worry. In Step #10, you will create a Grab & Go Checklist and your meds will be a priority item on that list. Or if you choose not to make an emergency medicine kit but instead plan to just have it as a priority item on your Grab & Go checklist, plan for it now.

Add pet medications here or in Step #9.

As for your pets' medicines, check out Step #9 to ensure you're prepared for their needs during an emergency.

Each year you will go through your emergency kit and your emergency supplies to check on outdated items, resupply anything you may have used, and add anything more you need. When it comes to medicines, one of the first questions is, should you keep or toss it if it's past the expiration date?

KEEP OR TOSS EXPIRED MEDICATION

Expiration dates may not necessarily mean you need to toss it. Here are a few rules of thumb:

Toss expired meds if your life depends on it.

Toss if it has changed color, consistency, or odor.

Toss = dispose of properly

- If your life depends on it — toss expired medication.

- If it has changed color, consistency or odor — toss it regardless of expiration.

- Don't take the aspirin if it smells like vinegar. It's one medication that should always be tossed when expired, or sooner if it smells like vinegar.

- Store medication in a cool, dry environment. Your bathroom medicine cabinet is rarely a good place.

For more information on expiration dates and medicine, check out this article from the Harvard Medical School Family Health Guide, www.health.harvard.edu/staying-healthy/drug-expiration-dates-do-they-mean-anything.

DISPOSING OF YOUR MEDICINE PROPERLY

The unused or expired prescription medication pushed to the back of your medicine cabinet is a safety concern. Disposing of your unused drugs properly can save lives and prevent accidental poisoning or misuse. It also protects the environment.

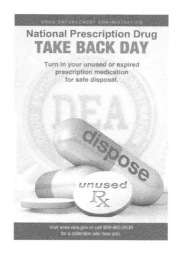

Check for a local medication disposal program, police department drop-box, pharmacy, or local medication take back event. You can do a web search for drug take back locations in your city or go directly to the Take Back Day website at takebackday.dea.gov. Contact the specific drop off location to confirm they can take your medicine. Most will not accept liquids or sharps. Many will take OTC (over-the-counter) medicine.

National Prescription Drug Take Back Day usually occurs in April and October. Check out takebackday.dea.gov to find a collection site near you. Many collection sites are local or state police stations and pharmacies.

Call your pharmacist for more information and to see if they participate in a drug take back program throughout the year. It's better to dispose of your prescription drugs throughout the year than to have them sitting in your medicine cabinet or drawer.

Use a local medication disposal program for your prescription meds.

Remove labels on the empty prescription bottles to protect your identity and information; the bottles can then be thrown away. Note: Though these bottles might come in handy someday, how many do you really need? Maybe just two or three. Not every single one, so don't save these for *a someday maybe* reason.

Most OTC and Rx meds that aren't collected can be thrown in the household trash.

Most OTC (over-the-counter) medications and Rx (prescription drugs) that aren't collected can be thrown in the household trash, but make sure they are less appealing to children and pets. Place the medication to be thrown away in a leak-proof container such as a sealable bag or empty laundry detergent bottle. Add coffee grounds or used kitty litter, seal, and toss.

Make it unappealing by adding used coffee grounds or kitty litter in a leak-proof container.

Do NOT flush your expired or unused medication down the toilet unless specifically instructed to do so by the drug label or

Disposing of your unused drugs properly can save lives and prevent accidental poisoning or misuse. It also protects the environment.

patient information provided. Only a few drugs carry instructions for flushing. Flushing medication can cause water pollution, have adverse effects on septic systems and may not be fully treated in sewage treatment plants.

For more information on proper disposal of your unused medicine:

- EPA (U.S. Environmental Protection Agency), *How to Dispose of Medicines Properly* www.epa.gov/sites/production/files/2015-06/documents/how-to-dispose-medicines.pdf

- FDA (U.S. Food and Drug Administration), *How to Dispose of Unused Medicines or Disposal of Unused Medicines: What You Should Know* www.fda.gov/ForConsumers/ConsumerUpdates/ucm101653.htm

SUMMARY

Pick ONE action to take today:

- ❑ Check with your insurance company about getting more than a 30-day supply of your daily medicine

- ❑ Build the habit of ordering your prescription medicine before you get down to the last couple of pills

- ❑ Build an emergency Rx and OTC supply

Possible Next Actions:

- ❑ Add a list of medicine (Rx and OTC) to your Grab & Go list (Step #10)

- ❑ Ask your pharmacist about unused drug disposal programs or find a drug take back location in your community

Resources

- • Expiration dates: www.health.harvard.edu/staying-healthy/drug-expiration-dates-do-they-mean-anything

- • Local drug take back locations: takebackday.dea.gov

- • Disposal: www.epa.gov/sites/production/files/2015-06/documents/how-to-dispose-medicines.pdf

- • Disposal: www.fda.gov/ForConsumers/Consumer Updates/ucm101653.htm

Add Notes Here ⬂

ONE action today

- ❑ Check with your insurance company about getting more than a 30-day supply of your daily medicine

- ❑ Build the habit of ordering your prescription medicine before you get down to the last couple of pills

- ❑ Build an emergency Rx and OTC supply

Build an Emergency Kit —Clothes and Hygiene

All the strength you need to achieve anything is within you.

Sara Henderson

Your emergency kit is intended to be the first thing you grab if you have to evacuate your home, or as a basic supply kit in your car if you can't get home. Which means you need some clothes and basic personal hygiene items.

Start with an extra pair of underwear and socks. It's amazing what you can handle next if you have a clean pair of your own underwear. You're not packing for a 2-week vacation so keep it to the minimum. An extra t-shirt or two, one pair of shorts and one pair of jeans, khakis, or other durable work pants. A light sweater or sweatshirt if you have room.

Do an annual review of the clothes in your kit. Wash if they're smelling musty and change them out if they no longer fit.

These clothes will not be a normal part of your wardrobe once you pack them in your emergency kit. You'll want to check the kit annually to make sure they're in good condition and fit (not too small and not too large). You will also want to wash the clothes to prevent them from smelling stale or musty. You probably won't want to pack away your favorite shirt, but you don't want to pull out a set of grungy jeans, either. I suggest using your favorite-but-too-old-to-really-wear-in-public clothes. Patch the jeans you've worn holes in and add them to your bag. That soft, comfortable t-shirt that is too faded — toss it in, too!

Add a pair of flip-flops to your kit. If you're staying at a shelter or even camping at a campground, a pair of flip-flops can be comfortable indoor shoes and provide protection for your feet from fungus in communal showers.

Add a t-shirt and yoga pants or another outfit for sleeping.

Regardless of what you normally sleep in, include clothes for sleeping that you won't mind hundreds of other people seeing you wear if you're staying at an evacuation shelter. One of your t-shirts and some lounging pants might work.

If you live in a place that gets cold or snows, add warmer items like sweat pants, long-sleeved shirts, and warm socks.

In addition to your clothes, pack a kit of personal hygiene items in travel size. Include:

- Shampoo, conditioner, soap, and lotion.

- Add a toothbrush, toothpaste. Does your dentist hand you a packet after a cleaning? Drop it in your kit.

- Feminine hygiene products if needed.

- Disposable shaver and cream.

- Include a wash cloth if you want and a "quick dry" towel. You may not normally use these but they'll be yours in an emergency shelter.

Add extra glasses like your old prescription glasses or cheaters.

Add an extra pair of glasses.

ONE action today

- ☐ Pack jeans and a t-shirt.
- ☐ Pack pajamas or clothes to sleep in.
- ☐ Add underwear and socks.
- ☐ Build a travel kit with personal hygiene items.
- ☐ Add Rx glasses or cheaters.

SUMMARY

Pick ONE action to take today:

- ☐ Pack jeans and a t-shirt.
- ☐ Pack pajamas or clothes to sleep in.
- ☐ Add underwear and socks to your emergency kit.
- ☐ Build a travel kit with personal hygiene items and add it to your emergency kit.
- ☐ Add Rx glasses or cheaters.

Possible Next Actions:

- ☐ If you don't already have a pair of walking shoes (and socks) in the car for those opportunities of getting extra steps in when you're out and about, add them now. In the winter, you'll want to have a pair of boots in the car as well.

- ☐ If you live in a place that gets cold or snows, add in warmer items. Consider a cold-weather car kit that includes a jacket, boots, a hat, scarf, gloves, and a blanket. You'll be prepared to shelter in your car if you're stuck on the road.

- ☐ Refer to Appendix A for a more detailed list of items to include in your emergency kit.

Add Notes Here ⬊

Prepare your Pets — Build an Emergency Supply Kit

During an emergency, whether it is localized to your family or extends to the wider community, you will want to ensure that your pets are taken care of, too. Build your emergency supply kit for pets.

Good preparation is better than hope for a miracle.

Sunday Adelaja

Though I'm sharing the complete kit list now, don't expect to complete it all at once. This is something you add to over time. Don't let the list overwhelm you so you do nothing. Use your normal purchasing of supplies to stock your emergency kit. For example, the next time you buy dog food (or hamster food), buy two. One will go in the house to restock and the other will be placed in your emergency supply kit.

When you're ready for another bag, you can buy one, move the "emergency supply" bag into the pet pantry and restock your kit with the new one. As with many of your supplies, you can pull from or "shop" your emergency supply shelf/container as long as you refill immediately.

"Shopping" your pet's emergency kit and refilling allows you to rotate supplies and keep them fresh.

Place the emergency supplies for your pets either in one container (airtight and waterproof if you can) or at least in one location. Though a large trash can isn't airtight, it can be big enough to hold most of the items and protect your supplies from minor water damage.

ITEMS TO PREPARE YOUR PETS FOR AN EMERGENCY:

Water (3-7 days). Your pet needs approximately 1 ounce of water per pound (of pet) per day. If your pet is 8 pounds, you'll need a cup a day. A one-gallon jug of water would be sufficient for a week. Your 60-pound dog will need a half-gallon of water a day, so you'll need 1.5 gallons for the first several days and 4 gallons would ensure enough for 7 days. This is an approximation which changes based on activity, weather, age, and stresses. The more active — the more water. The warmer the

Water: 1 ounce of water per pound (of pet)

weather — the more water. Check out Step #21 to learn more about water and emergency preparedness.

Food (3-7 days). Your bag of kibble will usually last longer than seven days if you're using this kit to restock your everyday supplies each time. Add canned food even if you routinely don't feed it to your pets. The canned food will have water in the food which can decrease the amount of water your pets will need to drink (and you need to store) for an emergency. The canned food will also be safer to use if flood waters impact your emergency supply kit — see Appendix L for proper handling of cans from floods.

Can Opener. If you include canned food in your pet's emergency supply kit, add a can opener.

Build the habit of refreshing your pet's medication in the emergency supply kit.

Medication (2 weeks). Even though your pet medications should be on your emergency Grab & Go checklist from Step #10 (those priority items you can't or won't put in an emergency kit), consider storing a supply of medicine here. Include flea and tick medication. Keep using and restocking the meds! Don't let them get old. Build the habit of stopping by your emergency supply kit when you bring home the new medicine and replace the emergency supply. Include a copy of the prescription in your vet records. Though only three to seven days (at a minimum) of food and water are suggested for this kit, you should plan on having two weeks of medication. Pet medication may not be a priority during the first days of an emergency.

Get a first aid book for pets. If you want an ebook get a print version as well.

First Aid book for pets. I like *The First-Aid Companion for Dogs & Cats* as it contains information on over-the-counter medication you can use (and which ones aren't safe for your pets), first-aid techniques, and a guide to common injuries and conditions. I recommend having both a print book and an ebook if you can. If you have to choose only one format, go with the print version. You won't need electricity to read it. There are also apps for your phone and tablet, but I've found that a book has more details and is more helpful. One app I tried kept telling me to go to my vet for everything.

First Aid Kit. Create a special pet first aid kit or add pet items to your main kit. Refer to your first aid book for an extensive list of items to have or search the internet using keywords such as "pet first aid kit list".

In general, you'll want to have supplies to respond to:

Routine care needs:

- ❑ Nail clippers

- ❑ Styptic powder

- ❑ Scissors, round tipped

- ❑ Tweezers or needle-nose pliers

- ❑ Tick removal tool (I like the Tick Key™ for ease of use on a squirming cat or dog)

Cuts, abrasions, foreign objects:

- ❑ Sterile saline solution

- ❑ Non-latex disposable gloves

- ❑ Cotton balls or swabs

- ❑ Antiseptic wipes, lotions, or spray

- ❑ Antibiotic ointment

- ❑ Gauze and non-stick bandages (self-sticking wrap)

Broken or sprained limbs

- ❑ Splints, tongue depressors, bubble wrap

- ❑ Self-sticking wrap, adhesive tape, even duct tape (to hold the splint in place — but don't get any hair stuck)

- ❑ Ice packs

Poisoning, allergic reactions — CALL VET or POISON CONTROL to confirm use, but have on hand

❏ Diphenhydramine (Benadryl®) for allergic reactions

❏ Hydrogen peroxide, 3%, if the vet or poison-control expert directs you to induce vomiting

❏ Syrup of Ipecac, if the vet or poison-control expert directs you to induce vomiting

❏ Poison Control Number

In addition to your vet's contact information, you'll want to have the Poison Control Number for animals. Have a credit card ready as a fee will usually apply.

▪ ASPCA Animal Poison Control Center Phone Number: **(888) 426-4435** (there's a fee)

▪ Pet Poison Helpline: **855-764-7661** (there's a fee)

A note about paying a fee for the poison control call — these call centers are staffed 24/7 by experts experienced in toxicology and animals. There's no government funding like the human poison control center. Yes, the specialist on the other end of the line may direct you to your vet, but you'll have a case number to give your vet to reference.

Get a carrier or crate **for each** pet.

Travel bag, carrier, or crate (one for each pet). There are two reasons for having this item: to provide a safe space to shelter during a disaster, and to safely transport your animal. A safe space requires a sturdy cage or kennel with sufficient room for your pet. When we moved our dogs and cats from Hawai'i in 2014, we had to use IATA (International Air Transport Association) approved kennels. They're sturdier then a regular kennel (and a bit more expensive) but they'll last. IATA's

Traveler's Pet Corner will help you size your kennel for your pet, Guidance for Dimensions of Container, iata.org/whatwedo /cargo/live-animals/pets/Pages/index.aspx.

The kennel should be big enough for the dog to comfortably stand, turn around, and lie down. The cat kennels need to be big enough to hold a litter tray or other material to allow your cat to go to the bathroom in the kennel. You're not likely to leash your cat to go for a walk to urinate and defecate as you would your dog.

Add your pet's name, your name and your contact information to the kennel. Do this immediately, don't wait until you're in the middle of a disaster. The IATA approved kennels come with a label but consider making a larger label that can be seen easily. If you don't want to write directly on the kennel with a permanent marker find labels or pouches that you can affix. Make sure they are water resistant.

You might also consider a smaller carrier if you're just transporting a small animal. A kennel big enough to comfortably house your cat or dog is usually too big or cumbersome to transport them to the vet or away from the disaster.

See Step #20 for more information and a general reminder on how to crate train your animals to make it a safe cave instead of a prison.

Anti-anxiety vest or wrap. Often referred to as a Thundershirt®, one specific brand, these anti-anxiety vests can help calm your dog or cat (and I'm assuming other pets as well) during a highly stressful time.

For a do-it-yourself wrap (which works!), use a scarf, long narrow strip of cloth, or a stretch bandage like Ace®. Place the middle of the scarf (cloth or bandage) on the front chest of your pet, wrap both ends up and over the animal's shoulders and back (the withers). Then bring the wrap down under the chest behind the front legs (the girth). If your scarf or cloth is long enough, cross the ends around the belly and back up to tie on the back. If the scarf isn't long enough, tying off under the belly will still

Anti-anxiety wrap

1. Across the chest

2. Over the shoulders

3. Under the chest

4. Over the back and tie (off the spine)

Keep your contact information current on tags.

provide comfort to your pet. Within seconds my large dog is calmer and will even fall asleep during a thunderstorm.

Even the self-sticking wrap bandages can be used if you have nothing else. You'll just start at one end and make the same general wrapping pattern, just not with two ends.

Another option is pet calming pheromone products. You can get them as a spray, diffuser, or collar. The pheromone products are species specific but are safe for humans and other species.

Collar/Harness and leash with Tags (cats/dogs). The next time you replace a collar or leash that's still in good condition, add it to your emergency kit instead of giving it away or throwing it away. Keep your old tags on the collar IF YOUR CONTACT NUMBER IS STILL CURRENT.

Which reminds me, are your tags current? Is your contact information the same? Get new ones immediately and double the order (one for your everyday collar and one for your emergency collar). Out-of-date information can delay your pet being safely returned to you if they're lost. And yes, have a harness and leash for your cat. Even though your cat may not like the leash and harness at first, it allows you to take the cat out of the kennel for a little exercise but still remain under your control. A harness is preferred to collars as it's harder to squirm out of a harness than it is a collar.

Muzzle. Even if your dog doesn't normally bite, in times of stress, you don't want your animal reacting instinctively and hurting you, anyone else or another animal. If you don't have a muzzle, another leash can be used. Take time now to search on YouTube to look at creating an emergency muzzle or learn how to get your dog used to a muzzle. Here's one I found — Emergency Dog Muzzle, youtu.be/h8CwNyfaU3g.

Long leash and yard stake (dogs). During an emergency or disaster, keep your pets under control at all. Under normal circumstances your dog may remain in the yard or under your voice control with no problems. But when you're stressed, your dog is stressed. Help them stay with you by keeping them on a leash at all times. The long leash and yard stake allows the dog to move about freely but still be contained. However, if your dog routinely breaks the line or pulls up the stake, you'll have to be prepared and add what will work for you and your dog.

Litter tray and litter (cats). Since it's less likely that your cat will walk on a leash and harness to use the bathroom, you'll need to have some material (newspapers, litter, etc.) in the kennel for your cat. Aluminum roasting pans make great disposable litter boxes. Litter can be used for other purposes too.

Add any additional sanitation and hygiene supplies you need to keep the crates and the area clean, such as trash bags and bleach.

Poop bags (dogs). You'll need to clean up after your dog, especially if you've had to evacuate to a shelter area. The fold top sandwich bags are great for pooper scoopers. Add those and some plastic shopping bags or small trash bags to your kit. Also add paper towels and spray disinfectant for animal waste cleanup.

Food and Water bowls. Regular bowls might take up too much space or add weight which you don't want to carry. Consider multi-purpose plastic food containers, collapsible pet bowls, or even a Frisbee®. Those flying discs can be purchased cheap, have a lip to hold water or food, and are rugged. They can also be used as a toy if your pet likes that kind of thing. But don't let them chew on them unless it's made for it.

Bedding. You probably won't have room for a second set of bedding material, but keep a car blanket, terry bath rugs, or towels handy to put in the kennels.

Toys and Treats. Your pet may be too stressed to play initially, but be prepared to offer a return to normalcy by having a toy, chews, or treats available when they're ready. It can help both of you regain your balance.

Note: I've suggested three to seven days of food and water. If you have room to store the supplies, consider increasing that to two weeks. Three days is a minimum to allow you to recover from the initial emergency. If the emergency or disaster is widespread, relief efforts may take longer to get to you. Start with three and add as you have the space and resources.

Start with 3 to 7 days' worth of supplies. If you have the space increase that to 2 weeks.

I've mentioned that you should keep your pet under control at all times during an emergency or disaster. If your pet gets scared, it may run away from you and the safe place you've come to. Don't add to your worry and stress by having to search for a lost pet after you're safely away from the emergency or disaster area. Even if you shelter in place, you'll want to ensure your animals can't get out and get lost. Keep animals inside unless on a leash or inside a well-maintained physical fence.

RECORDS TO PUT IN YOUR KIT

Vet records. Include vaccination records, particularly rabies, and any special instructions or health concerns. Highlight the description of your pet (breed, weight, coloring, etc.) to find it quickly if you need to give a description of your pet. Sure, you know what they look like, but your vet may describe them differently.

Vet contact information. It's probably in your contacts already, but add it to your paper and paperless records.

Recent photo of pet. It's likely you have several (if not a thousand) pet photos on your phone. Print several. Include photos from different sides and show any special marking, like that back paw that is white or the tip of the tail that's black, etc. Get items in the background that can help determine actual size of the pet. A chair can help the authorities know whether your dog is 10 pounds of attitude or 50 pounds of fluff.

Microchip records. Refer to Step #16 for details on microchipping. Be sure to update your information and include it with your emergency kit paperwork. Your local humane society may be able to help with updating the information or you may have to contact the manufacturer.

Other Vital Documents, such as adoption papers and proof of ownership. Add anything you think the authorities might need to reunite you with a lost pet.

Detailed Care Instructions. In case you are unable to care for your pet, include special feeding, medication, and care instructions. If your dog needs a grain-free diet, or your cat needs medicine, or your bird needs to be covered at night, write it down and include it in your kit.

You may choose to go paperless for most situations, but for these items, use both paper and paperless copies so you can access the information regardless of emergency conditions. After all, you're preparing for an emergency or a disaster and you don't know whether the electricity and the internet will be working in your area.

Place the print copy of the records in a waterproof bag. Though most manufacturers of the reclosable zipper bags, like Ziploc®, will not call these bags waterproof, they're a good start until you can get waterproof bags in your emergency kit (if you choose to). I personally use the freezer bags and double bag. It's not guaranteed, but it's a start.

Scan or snap a picture of these documents and keep the paperless copy in the cloud application you prefer such as Dropbox, Box, Google Drive. Keep another copy in a note-taking app such as Evernote*, OneNote, or Google Keep for easy access and sharing on your phone or tablet. I prefer Dropbox and Evernote, but I've used them all. Share your cloud folder and your notebook with trusted family members or friends. Give access to this information to at least one person who lives outside of the state. Refer to Step #15 for your check-in plan. We'll discuss electronic documents and backups in Step #27 in more detail.

Though I mentioned only dogs and cats, preparing for emergencies and disasters applies for all your animals. For specific information on birds, reptiles, horses, and small animals check out the American Society for the Prevention of Cruelty to Animals' (ASPCA's) article, Disaster Preparedness, www.aspca.org/pet-care/general-pet-care/disaster-preparedness.

A checklist of the items listed above can be found in Appendix B or download a copy at www.dhucks.com/resources-31-smallsteps-emergencies.

Go **paper and digital** for key documents. Be prepared for power and internet outages.

Put the papers in a waterproof bag.

Emergency Kit for Pets

ONE action today

- ☐ Get a container to hold your pet's supplies.

- ☐ Start building your pet emergency kit.

- ☐ Make "shopping" your pet's emergency kit a habit.

- ☐ Buy a pet first aid book in print.

- ☐ Add the animal poison control number to your phone

SUMMARY

Pick ONE action to take today:

- ☐ Get a container to hold your pet's emergency supplies.

- ☐ Start building your pet emergency kit. Add to it over time.

- ☐ Make pulling from and restocking your pet's emergency kit a habit — "shop" your emergency kit. This rotates the supplies and keeps food and medication fresh.

- ☐ Buy a pet first aid book. Choose a print version first.

- ☐ Add the animal poison control number to your phone list.

Possible Next Actions:

- ☐ Add one more item to your pet's emergency kit.

- ☐ Check the contact information on your pet's tag. Update if necessary.

- ☐ Keep a leash in your vehicle. If you frequently travel with your dog in the car, keep a leash in the vehicle in case you have to vacate the car.

- ☐ Make a copy of your pet's records (vaccinations, microchip number, medicine, dietary needs) and keep a copy with the pet emergency supply kit.

Resources:

- Dimensions for container: www.iata.org/whatwedo /cargo/live-animals/pets/Pages/index.aspx

- Emergency muzzle: youtu.be/h8CwNyfaU3g

- Birds, reptiles, horses, and small animals: www.aspca.org/pet-care/general-pet-care/disaster-preparedness

- Download checklist: www.dhucks.com/resources-31-smallsteps-emergencies.

Add Notes Here ⬊

10 Create Your Grab & Go Checklist

Things which matter most must never be at the mercy of those that matter the least.

Johann Wolfgang von Goethe

Don't rely on your memory during an emergency or a disaster. When you and your adrenaline are rushing through the house, your brain is focused on 'fight or flight' not whether or not you need to take the toothpaste or grab the extra batteries. Use a Grab & Go checklist.

There will always be more items than your emergency kit can hold, and you will want to take more with you during an evacuation. Now is the time to create your Grab & Go Checklist.

Start with the checklist of items I provide at the end of this Step (same list as in Appendix C). Add other items as you think of them. Before we get to the list, consider the tool(s) you'll use to create the list. You could:

Don't rely on your memory during an emergency or a disaster. Make a checklist for things to **grab** and **go** if you need to evacuate.

- Write the list on paper and add it to your PIC (Personal Information Center) from Step #11. Expect to rewrite it several times because you will want to prioritize the items.

- Use a word processing program and print out a copy to add to your PIC (Step #11) and keep an electronic copy. (MS Word, Apache OpenOffice Writer, LibreOffice Writer, Google Docs)

- A spreadsheet would allow you to easily reorganize items based on the priority you set. (MS Excel, Apache OpenOffice Calc, LibreOffice Calc, Google Sheets)

- Note taking apps like Evernote, OneNote or Google have check boxes you can easily click and unclick on your smartphone.

  If you use Evernote (or other checklist tool) for your checklists, make sure you have the version that allows you access to your checklists when you are offline.

You'll also need to consider whether you want a paper copy to check off or prefer an electronic copy to mark collected items. If you're comfortable with technology, I recommend both. A paper list in your PIC that anyone in your family can access and an electronic list on your smartphone or tablet. Depending on the platform, you could share it with your family as well.

Again, if you go with an electronic checklist or document, make sure you can access it offline if the power and your internet go down.

If you're going digital, make sure you can access your checklist if you don't have power or internet access.

Make several copies of the paper checklist. Add one to the front of your PIC when you get to Step #11. Place one in your emergency kit (Step #6), one in your camping gear (Step #23), which could be a great reminder of what to pack for camping, and one in your pet's emergency kit (Step #9). Add a copy in any other location you can think of, such as your cooler, pantry, or luggage.

On the next page (and in Appendix C) is an example list of items to include in you Grab & Go Checklist. If you would like a copy of my list go to www.dhucks.com/resources-31-smallsteps-emergencies and download a PDF copy.

Grab & Go Checklist

GRAB

Priority Items

- ❑ Emergency Cash
- ❑ PIC Notebook
- ❑ Bill paying kit
- ❑ Passports & IDs
- ❑ Safety deposit key or home safe

Electronics

- ❑ Phones
- ❑ Phone chargers
- ❑ Batteries
- ❑ Flashlights & Lanterns
- ❑ Laptops & power cords
- ❑ iPads/Tablets & chargers
- ❑ Portable charger pack
- ❑ Camera & charger

Medication

- ❑ Prescription medication
- ❑ Any written prescriptions
- ❑ Medical equipment
- ❑ Pet medication
- ❑ Cold, Flu & Allergy medication
- ❑ Ibuprofen/Aspirin /Acetaminophen
- ❑ Supplements

PREP

Priority Items

- ❑ Gas up
- ❑ ATM — more cash
- ❑ Buy extra batteries

Electronics (if time)

- ❑ Charge phones
- ❑ Charge laptops
- ❑ Charge tablets
- ❑ Charge portable charger pack
- ❑ Forward home phone to cell phone, if applicable

Medication

- ❑ Charge batteries for medical equipment

GRAB	**PREP**

Clothing (GRAB)

- ❑ Luggage
- ❑ Jeans, 1-2
- ❑ T-shirts, 1-2
- ❑ Long-sleeved shirt
- ❑ Pajamas
- ❑ Jacket or sweater
- ❑ Underwear
- ❑ Socks
- ❑ Walking shoes
- ❑ Flip flops
- ❑ Warm boots*
- ❑ Warm jacket*
- ❑ Hat and gloves*

Clothing (PREP)

* if winter

Comfort and Hygiene (GRAB)

- ❑ Pillows**
- ❑ Blankets** (or sleeping bag)
- ❑ Toothbrush and toothpaste
- ❑ Personal hygiene products
- ❑ Toilet paper
- ❑ Trash bags

Comfort and Hygiene (PREP)

** evacuation shelters may not have these

Dry Goods (GRAB)

- ❑ Coffee/Tea/Cocoa
- ❑ Sugar
- ❑ Canned meats
- ❑ Canned fruits
- ❑ Canned vegetables
- ❑ **Can opener**
- ❑ Peanut butter
- ❑ Crackers
- ❑ Individual snacks
- ❑ Water

Dry Goods (PREP)

- ❑ Fill water bottles

GRAB	**PREP**

Refrigerated and Frozen Foods

- ❏ Cooler(s)
- ❏ Reusable ice packs
- ❏ Frozen foods easily cooked
- ❏ Fruits and vegetables
- ❏ Deli meats
- ❏ Cheeses
- ❏ Refrigerated foods that are safe if unrefrigerated for 4 hours or more

Refrigerated and Frozen Foods

- ❏ Freeze all reusable ice packs
- ❏ Freeze additional bags or bottles of water, leave space for expansion
- ❏ Buy ice
- ❏ Put a thermometer in cooler to ensure safe temperatures are maintained***

*** refer to Appendix J (Refrigerated Foods) and Appendix K (Frozen Foods) for safe temperatures

SUMMARY

Pick ONE action to take today:

- ❑ Build your Grab & Go List

Possible Next Actions:

- ❑ Try the list out by using it for double duty. Use it for packing for vacations, camping trips, picnics.
- ❑ Purchase refrigerator-freezer thermometer to monitor temperature.

Resources:

- Download checklist: www.dhucks.com/resources-31-smallsteps-emergencies.

ONE action today

- ❑ Build your Grab & Go List

Add Notes Here ➘

Your Personal Information Center (PIC)

If you believe that feeling bad or worrying long enough will change a past or future event, then you are residing on another planet with a different reality system.

William James

Build your **Personal Information Center (PIC)** to be prepared for an emergency, organized for a move or keep your bills and financial information orderly every day.

Actually, before you can 'take your PIC' you have to make your PIC (Personal Information Center) notebook. Then you can add your Grab & Go Checklist (Step #10) and 'take your PIC' in an emergency.

Your PIC is a physical notebook or a digital file containing essential personal information and important records such as copies of utility bills, bank and credit card statements, medical history, wills, birth certificates, death certificates and other vital documents. The notebook makes it easier for you to collect all the important information on your family, home, finances, and medical in one place, so that in an emergency you can *Take Your PIC* and go.

The PIC isn't just for emergencies though. You can use it to stay organized during a routine move or bill paying. The PIC will even be a resource if the primary bill payer needs someone else to take care of the finances.

WHAT GOES IN THE PIC?

There will be three main sections to your PIC notebook.

1. **PLANS:** This section will be your first tab and contain:

   • Grab & Go checklist from Step #10;

   • your family communication plan and household information sheet which you'll build in Steps #14 and #15;

   • the emergency kit supply list from Step #6 (also in Appendix A);

   • and the emergency supply list for your pets from Step #9 (also in Appendix B).

2. **PHOTOS:** This section will be the second tab and contain:

- Up-to-date photos of family members and pets from Step #13; and

- The photos from the home inventory photos (Step #26) should stay with the inventory list of household items which will go under the **Property** tab in the **DOCUMENTS** section.

3. **DOCUMENTS:** There's not just one tab labeled "documents." This section is a series of tabs, one for each of the main categories below:

- **Bank Accounts**

- **Bills**

- **Credit Cards**

- **Digital Accounts**

- **Insurance**

- **Investments**

- **Medical**

- **Pets**

- **Property**

- **Safe Deposit Box**

- **Wills and Directives**

- any additional tabs you choose.

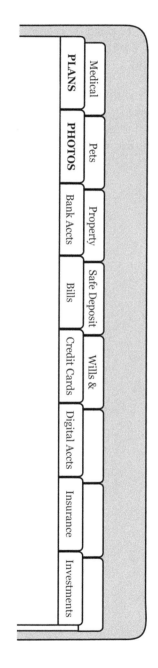

Before we get into specifics about the sections and documents to include, you'll have to decide whether you'll start building a hard copy (paper) notebook or an electronic file. You may create both

Building a complete PIC will take time, effort, and energy. You are not going to build it overnight or in one sitting.

Start with whichever format (print or digital) you find easiest to work with. But **START!**

eventually but start with the format you feel will be easiest for you.

IF YOU START WITH A HARD COPY, YOU'LL NEED:

- A 3-ring binder: heavy-duty, 2" or larger

- Write-on tab dividers

- Either an envelope or a plastic binder pocket

- Optional: sheet protectors

- 3-hole punch

I recommend a brightly colored notebook. It is easier to spot and remember to take when you evacuate (and more fun to build). There are other options rather than a notebook, such as an accordion file, but notebooks make it easier to find the paper you want and provides its own flat work surface. In general, notebooks only need two hands to work, while I've found that three hands are the minimum requirement for an accordion file — one to hold the document I'm adding, one to hold open the accordion file and a third one to keep the accordion file from falling over.

NOTE: If you want to use sheet protectors instead of or in addition to 3-hole punching the paper, purchase tab dividers and notebooks made specifically to hold sheet protectors. They are wider than the normal.

PREFER TO BUY A READY-MADE NOTEBOOK?

Some products are made specifically for organizing personal and household information. You can find them as file folders, accordion folders, or notebooks. They may be a great choice as you don't have to purchase the tabs and notebooks separately, but the downside is they may not be as flexible as you need them to be. You may not be able to add or change a tab so it better reflects your needs and situation.

Creating your own PIC allows you to make only the sections you need, change the name of a section to one you can remember better, and update the notebook at any time to something brighter, newer, or easier to use.

If you want to look at available ready-made products, use the search terms "important document organizer" or "emergency binder."

What you will be doing in this step is easier than other notebooks or files, which may require you to write or type in all the essential information. You will take your statement, bill, or important document, 3-hole punch it (or a COPY), and place it in your PIC notebook. Or you can save it digitally in your electronic PIC (ePIC).

IF YOU START WITH AN ELECTRONIC COPY, YOU'LL NEED:

A platform: Will it be Dropbox, Google Drive, or other cloud storage service? Will it be a note-taking app like Evernote? Is it secure enough? Can you easily scan a paper statement into your notebook? Will you be able to export the files or create a copy?

A scanner: Either a stand-alone scanner like ScanSnap from Fujitsu or the scanner in your all-in-one printer. There are even phone apps for that purpose (such as Genius Scan), and cloud storage services such as Dropbox are starting to include scanning capability in their mobile apps.

A naming system: Establish a file naming protocol to easily retrieve the document you want. Normally your electronic files

Take a look at the apps and tools you already have. There may be additional bells and whistles that may help you create your ePIC.

don't have to resemble a paper storage filing system (you name and organize your files differently) but in this case, I'd suggest you organize your ePIC in a similar manner to the paper notebook. We'll talk more on that in the next section.

PREFER TO BUY A READY-MADE PROGRAM OR APP?

There are products out there that can help you create something similar to a PIC. Some are specially formatted electronic platforms that are built for the function. The downsides are: you may have to pay an annual fee to maintain the information; you may not be able to export the data; or the app/software may not be maintained by the company in the future.

WHICH SHOULD YOU START WITH — PAPER OR ELECTRONIC?

It depends on your preference really, but here are a few pros and cons:

Paper:

Paper or electronic? There are pros and cons for each. Choose whichever one will get you started.

(Pro) Easier, less work to assemble, and potentially cheaper if you're not already scanning your documents every month.

(Pro) You're not dependent on your electronic devices working

(Pro) Others in your family can use it and refer to it regardless of computer experience

(Con) Bulkier and heavier to grab and evacuate.

(Security) Your PIC is as secure as your home and other personal information. Don't leave it laying around.

Electronic:

(Pro) Easier to access from anywhere and any device, depending on platform

(Pro) Takes up less space on your shelf

(Con) Requires power for your device and internet access depending on platform

(Security) Your ePIC is as secure as the rest of your files.

Now that you have an overview of the three sections and have decided to start with one format (either the print PIC or the ePIC), let's jump in to building your PIC.

BUILDING YOUR PIC

TAB #1 — PLANS

Add a tab and label it **PLANS**. As we discussed earlier you'll add:

- ❑ Your Grab & Go checklist from Step #10;

- ❑ Your family communication plan from Steps #14 and #15;

- ❑ The emergency kit supply list from Step #6 (also in Appendix A); and

- ❑ The emergency supply list for your pets from Step #9 (also in Appendix B).

Either 3-hole punch or scan each list and insert it in this section.

Add your Grab & Go checklist from Step #10. Then keep adding plans and checklists that will help you prepare and respond to an emergency.

TAB #2 — PHOTOS

Add a tab and label it **PHOTOS**.

If you have prints made, you'll need an envelope or closed binder pocket to put them in. But since most photos are taken on a phone these days, just print out the highest quality photos you can and 3-hole punch them for your notebook. Include family members living in the house and maybe nearby relatives. Your immediate focus may be your family, but maybe your relatives on the other side of the city, state or country are the ones you're looking for. You'll focus on getting updated pictures of your family and pets in Step #13 (Take Updated Photos), though I'm

Investments

Insurance

Digital Accts

Wills &

Credit Cards

Safe Deposit

Bills

Property

Bank Accts

Pets

PHOTOS

Medical

PLANS

sure you have some on your phone, on a computer, or as prints already.

Household inventory photos taken while creating a household inventory should go in the Property tab along with the list of household items. We'll look at household inventory in Step #26.

TABS #3 through#13 — DOCUMENTS

Add 11 tabs for the categories below and any additional tabs you choose.

- ❑ **Bank Accounts**
- ❑ **Bills**
- ❑ **Credit Cards**
- ❑ **Digital Accounts**
- ❑ **Insurance**
- ❑ **Investments**
- ❑ **Medical**
- ❑ **Pets**
- ❑ **Property**
- ❑ **Safe Deposit Box**
- ❑ **Wills and Directives**
- ❑ additional tabs you choose

As mentioned previously, the PIC notebook is easier than most other document products because you won't be rewriting or typing in account and contact information. You will:

- take your statements, bills, and important documents (or COPIES),
- 3-hole punch each one, and
- place it in your PIC notebook.
- Or you can scan and save it digitally to your ePIC.

Examples of the type of statements and documents which go in each category.

Bank Accounts

- ☐ Checking / Share Draft / NOW
- ☐ Savings / Share
- ☐ Cash, amounts and locations (savings deposit box, emergency kit, coffee can in the back yard)
- ☐ CDs
- ☐ Money market accounts
- ☐ Revolving lines of credit attached to your checking
- ☐ Savings bonds

Bills

- ☐ Auto Registration
- ☐ Home Maintenance — Pest Protection / Security / Lawn Care
- ☐ Insurance bills/payments (copies of the policies will go under the Insurance tab)
  - ☐ Auto
  - ☐ Dental
  - ☐ Homeowners
  - ☐ Life
  - ☐ Renters
  - ☐ Medical
- ☐ Loans
- ☐ Magazine Subscriptions (not as important, but why not). Cut off the cover with the mailing label and three-hole punch it. Add it to this section
- ☐ Mortgage / Rent
- ☐ Property taxes
- ☐ Utilities
  - ☐ Cable/Internet
  - ☐ Electricity
  - ☐ Gas
  - ☐ Phone (Cell, Landline)
  - ☐ Sewer
  - ☐ Trash
  - ☐ Water

Credit Cards

- ☐ American Express
- ☐ Discover
- ☐ Visa / MasterCard
- ☐ Department Stores (Sears, Macy's, etc.)
- ☐ Gas

Digital Accounts — details in Step #12

Insurance – include policy statements (the bill statements go under the Bills tab)

- ☐ Auto
- ☐ Home / Renters
- ☐ Medical
- ☐ Dental
- ☐ Eye
- ☐ Accident
- ☐ Disability
- ☐ Life
- ☐ Pet medical

Investments

- ☐ 401(k)s
- ☐ Bonds
- ☐ Brokerage Accounts
- ☐ Businesses
- ☐ DRIPs
- ☐ IRAs
- ☐ Partnerships
- ☐ Retirement

Medical – you need a list of doctors, prescriptions, medical equipment, and provider contact information for every family member, but instead of writing all that down, add the Explanation of Benefits (EOB) report that your insurance provides or the doctor and facility bill statement.

- ❑ Primary care
- ❑ Specialists
- ❑ Dental
- ❑ Eye
- ❑ Home care
- ❑ Meals assistance
- ❑ Pharmacy — receipts and prescription information
- ❑ Medical equipment — receipts, maintenance or service agreements, operating instructions, repair and replacement information
- ❑ Allergies or health issues
- ❑ Recurring appointments (dialysis, oncology treatment, therapy, etc.)
- ❑ Vaccination records
- ❑ **Date of last Tetanus shot** _____

Pets

- ❑ Latest vet bill with vaccinations
- ❑ Health needs — receipts, vet bills, etc.
  - ❑ Allergies
  - ❑ Dietary needs
  - ❑ Medication
  - ❑ Treatments
- ❑ Microchip certificate
- ❑ Receipt from Pet Recovery Service
- ❑ Receipt from your pet sitter or day-care
- ❑ Photos of your pets (if you want additional ones here)

Property

☐ Property inventory list (aka home inventory, Step #26)

☐ Receipts for art or other big-ticket items

☐ Vehicle registrations (a copy of course or an old one)

☐ Other documentation

Safe Deposit Box – add a copy to your PIC

☐ Birth certificates

☐ Death certificates

☐ Deeds

☐ Digital accounts list (Step #12)

☐ Divorce certificates

☐ Irreplaceable memorabilia

☐ Life insurance policies

☐ Passports

☐ Property inventory (include photos, video, certificate of ownership, etc.)

☐ Retirement Account Information

☐ Social Security cards

☐ Wedding certificates

Add a list of other items you have in your safe deposit box

☐ _____

☐ _____

☐ _____

Add:

☐ Location of safe deposit box

☐ Location of safe deposit box key

☐ Box #:

☐ Signatories

☐ Security requirements

If you don't have a safe deposit box consider a fire safe. Review the manufacturer's details. Each model will have a different fire rating (how long the contents will be safe at a certain temperature). In addition, look for models that will protect from water damage. The description will state how long and to what depth the safes are rated for.

Wills and Directives

- ❐ Last Will and Testament
- ❐ Health Care Advance Directive
- ❐ Power-of-Attorney
- ❐ Trusts
- ❐ Location of originals: _____

The original copies should be kept in a safe place. A safe deposit box is not a good place for wills or directives as your executor may not be able to access it unless they are signatories on the box.

Download checklists at www.dhucks.com/resources-31-smallsteps-emergencies

ADDITIONAL INFORMATION TO INCLUDE

Some information on a statement or bill might be important enough to highlight or you may have to write it on the statement. If you have an electronic PIC (ePIC) with PDF statements, use the PDF Fill & Sign feature or create a separate text file to add the information. Information such as:

- ✔ Account number
- ✔ Contact information (phone, website, address)
- ✔ Who is on the account, if not shown
- ✔ Beneficiary, if appropriate
- ✔ How you receive your statement (mail or email /electronic)
- ✔ How you access your account (check, ATM, phone, internet)
- ✔ How you pay the bill (check, automatic payment, on-line
- ✔ Intent for the account (vacation, business, 6-month emergency fund, etc.)

- ✔ How often and when the bill is due (monthly on the 5th, every 3 months, annually)
- ✔ Specific health issues
- ✔ Foods requirements (Pet tab)
- ✔ Purchase dates
- ✔ Add other details you want to include

The goal is to continue to build your PIC over time, just like your cash stash and your emergency supplies.

You don't have to collect ALL this information today. Plan to add the various statements and copies over the next three months. As you pay your bills, instead of filing (or shredding/tossing) your statements, 3-hole punch a statement, add it to the appropriate section. Jot down the additional information you need or highlight the information.

You might get most of it done in the first month, but if there are non-monthly bills or accounts, you should be able to collect the majority within three months. You won't be adding every statement every month.

Before you leave this step, schedule an annual review in your calendar now. You won't necessarily replace all your statements, bills, and records. You'll check what you have, update what you need, and add anything that's missing.

Check that your address, email, phone number and other important contact information are up-to-date with each account. You might even check it this year as you add each statement. Yes, that will mean more time in the bill paying mode, but preparing now will mean less stress in an emergency and possible prevention of late fees due to an inability to contact you.

Keep your information secure.

Add a 2-gallon reclosable plastic bag to your PIC or your emergency kit. If you're evacuating, place your PIC in the bag to keep it dry.

Keep your hard copy PIC notebook and your ePIC secure.

Due to possible identify theft, writing down your username and password, as well as security questions, has not been recommended. However, since each account should have a unique password, and each password should be at least 12 characters long, it is next to impossible (at least for me) to remember all the passwords. Since we are talking passwords here, another recommendation for keeping your accounts secure is to make your password a sentence (again at least 12 characters long). Keep the phrase positive or uplifting. Might as well give yourself a mental lift while you're paying those bills.

If you have trouble remembering your passwords or questions, you could include it here in your PIC if you feel it is appropriate. Keep the hard copy notebook and the ePIC as secure as you would other personal and financial information.

If you write down your passwords DON'T keep the list next to your computer. If you include usernames and passwords along with other financial information in this PIC, don't label the notebook "Personal Information," PIC will do. Or keep it unlabeled. Store your PIC in a secure location that is easy for you to grab but not for others to gain access to it.

Keep your usernames and passwords secure. If you keep them on paper, DON'T keep them next to your computer.

If you're comfortable with electronic information, there are two password manager apps I recommend: 1Password (1password.com) and LastPass (www.lastpass.com). To find the current "best" password manager, use the search term "best password manger" or something similar and look through the articles written by reputable sites.

For more ways to keep your accounts secure and stay safe online go to staysafeonline.org/stay-safe-online/securing-key-accounts-devices/passwords-securing-accounts. The National Cyber Security Alliance website, staysafeonline.org, has other online safety tips and resources. Check it out.

ONE action today

- ❑ Get a notebook and set of tabs. Start building your PIC.

- ❑ Choose an electronic platform and start build your electronic PIC (ePIC)

SUMMARY

Pick ONE action to take today:

- ❑ Get a notebook and set of tabs. Start building your PIC.

- ❑ Choose an electronic platform and start build your electronic PIC (ePIC)

Possible Next Actions:

- ❑ Get a safe deposit box

- ❑ Get a fire and water-resistant home safe

- ❑ Update your Will. If you don't have one, get one.

- ❑ Update your Health Care Advance Directive (Living Will). If you don't have one, get one.

Resources:

- • Download checklist: www.dhucks.com/resources-31-smallsteps-emergencies.

- • Password manager: 1password.com

- • Password manager: www.lastpass.com

- • How to stay safe online: staysafeonline.org/stay-safe-online/securing-key-accounts-devices/passwords-securing-accounts

Keep your hard copy PIC notebook and your ePIC secure

Add Notes Here ⬊

Your Digital Accounts — List Them

As you created your PIC (Step #11), you added your bank accounts, utility bills, and maybe even remembered to include your twice annual car insurance bill. But you may not have thought to include your email and social media accounts or the numerous apps you've added to your smartphone over the years. Even if you're one of the 13% of Americans who don't use the Internet,[3] it's still possible you have an email address. You may have a Facebook account to stay in touch with the grandchildren. Or you may have a Skype account to talk with distant family members.

In this Step, you'll create a list of all the online/internet accounts you have that you didn't already include in your PIC. It could be in paper or digital form, but it should be stored in a secure place because it will include your usernames and passwords. You can add this list to your PIC (Step #11) under the **Digital Accounts** tab or just note the location of the list under the tab. As with your PIC, you'll add to it over time as you remember old accounts or create new accounts.

Include the following information for each account on your list:

- Name of Account

- Website URL

- Payment information. Include how often you're charged, how you pay (credit card, bank account, invoiced, or automatic debit, etc.)

- If you access the account from an app on your phone, tablet or computer, note which device and app name.

- Use or reason for the account, i.e. personal email, social media page for business, emergency fund, receive payment from..., etc.

- Additional individuals on the account or with account access.

Confidence sometimes requires purposeful preparation and practice.

Sam Owen

Keep your usernames and passwords secure. Either in a password manager app or on paper that is stored away from your computer.

You will also need to include the usernames and passwords for each account, either on the list itself (KEEP IT SECURE), in a password manager app, such as 1Password or LastPass, or a separate list that you keep in a safe deposit box or other secure location. Reminder: each account should have a strong and unique password.

And, just like your PIC, this list isn't only for emergencies. You'll use this list if you need someone else to help you take care of your accounts.

Examples of service and product accounts to include are:

- ❑ Data storage (Dropbox, Box, Google Drive, iCloud, OneDrive, backup applications, computers, external hard drives, etc.)

- ❑ Devices (computers, laptops, phone, tablet, etc.). Though these may not be "accounts", you might use a password to lock the device. And they definitely contain data. Include these.

- ❑ Email (Gmail, Yahoo, Outlook etc.)

- ❑ Entertainment (Netflix, Acorn, Vudu, Hulu, Amazon, CBS, NBC, ABC, etc.)

- ❑ Home inventory (spreadsheet on your computer, an app on your phone, or an account on the web, etc.). The paper version of your home inventory list would be located behind the **Property** tab in your PIC.

- ❑ Photo storage and organizing accounts (Google, iCloud, Costco, Forever, Dropbox, etc.)

- ❑ Shopping accounts (Amazon, eBay, Etsy, etc.)

- ❑ Social Media (Facebook, Twitter, Snapchat, Goodreads, Instagram, Pinterest, Google+, etc.) Note if your credit card or bank account is attached.

- ❑ Utilities (internet, phone, cell phone, etc.) if you didn't already include them in your PIC under the **Bills** tab

- ❑ Websites, blogs, and domains you own

Include financial accounts if you didn't already include them in your PIC under the **Bank Accounts** and **Investments** tabs. Accounts such as:

❑ Bank Accounts

❑ Investment accounts

❑ Retirement Accounts

You may also have additional assets to list:

❑ Books you've published (CreateSpace, KDP, iTunes, Barnes & Noble Nook, Kobo, Smashwords, Amazon Author Page, Ingram, publishers, agent, etc.).

❑ eCommerce sites for your products, services, creations, and more (eBay, Etsy, auction sites, online art galleries, classified ad sites such as Craigslist, etc.).

❑ Income producing accounts that provide passive income (affiliates programs, YouTube, online training sites, etc.).

❑ Merchant accounts (PayPal, QuickBooks, Square, etc.).

❑ Social Media (Facebook, Snapchat, Instagram, etc.). Yes, social media accounts may have income associated with them. Did you set up a Buy button on your business page or use the peer-to-peer (P2P) payment system to get the cost of that ticket from your friend? Note it.

Also record if the accounts automatically transfer the money to your bank account or if it has to be done manually. Include which accounts are connected.

ONE action today

- ❑ Decide —Paper or Electronic list of digital accounts and how you'll keep it secure.

- ❑ Start your list

- ❑ Add to your list

SUMMARY

Pick ONE action to take today:

- ❑ Decide whether you're going digital or paper with your list of digital accounts and how you'll keep the information secure.

- ❑ Start your list of accounts. Keep it secure. ☺

- ❑ Add to your list of accounts. Keep it secure. ☺ ☺

Possible Next Actions:

- ❑ Go to Appendix D — Digital Estate Planning to learn about assigning legacy contacts, inactive account managers, and other options for developing a Digital Estate Plan.

Add Notes Here ⬂

Take Updated Photos of Family and Pets

If you have a smartphone, you probably have lots of photos of your family and your pets on it. But these photos may not be what you need in an emergency if you're searching for missing family members or lost pets.

For your family, take pictures of your family members from several different angles. Take a picture with them standing next to a door to get a sense of their height. Snap a picture in profile. This isn't a mug shot so you can have fun with this. Let them know this isn't for sharing on Facebook or Instagram but for preparedness. Make sure the pictures are in focus and up close enough to see details. Avoid busy or distracting backgrounds.

The same goes for pets. Get pictures of them from the sides, front, and back. Place them next to a chair, door, or other item that will help in estimating the size of the animal. Get a picture of any distinguishing marks like a white paw or orange spot over the eye.

If you already have good photos, use those.

Next, collect these photos into one electronic folder and make copies of the folder. The more places you have these photos, the easier it will be to ensure they're available when you need them. Have copies on your phone that you can text out if needed. Keep copies in the cloud so you can print out the pictures. I'd also suggest having copies in a note taking app like Evernote. If you have a premium Evernote account, you can keep the notebook offline accessible. Share the notebook and folder files with your family members and your out-of-town contact.

Print out a copy of each photo and include them in your print PIC. The goal here is to have photos ready to create posters or to

Good luck is a residue of preparation.

Jack Youngblood

When taking photos, place family and pets next to familiar objects such as doors, chairs. This gives an idea of height and size.

give to the emergency responders who might be helping you find your loved one or your pet.

If you don't have a smartphone with a camera or a digital camera, purchase a disposable camera and start snapping. Once you've taken enough pictures (one or two rolls should be sufficient) make it a priority to get them processed and placed in your PIC (Step #11).

SUMMARY

Pick ONE action to take today:

- ❑ Take pictures of your pets and family members.

- ❑ Print out a few pictures and add to your PIC (Step #11)

Add Notes Here ↘

ONE action today

- ❑ Take pictures of your pets and family members.

- ❑ Print out a few pictures and add to your PIC

14

Make a Plan — Meetup

Emergencies and disasters don't wait for your family to be together. Sometimes you may have days to plan and prepare, such as before a hurricane or winter storm *watch* turns into a *warning*4. But other times a disaster may hit while you're going about your daily life. You're at work, shopping, at the doctors, or maybe even at the gym. Your kids may be at school, your parents may be visiting friends, and your spouse, partner or roommate may be out and about doing their thing. If something happens in your neighborhood and you need to evacuate, where will you meet if you can't meet at home?

By discussing *what-if* scenarios based on your top three hazards you can identify locations, accommodations, and challenges. Think about where you could meet if you needed to evacuate your home in your car. Where could you meet if you had to evacuate on foot? If you don't have a car, how will you evacuate? Discuss with family, friends and neighbors the help you'll need if you have to evacuate.

What if you needed to leave your place of work? Your workplace evacuation plan may require you meet at a designated spot for accountability, but then what? What if you can't get back into work and have to leave? On foot? In your vehicle? On the bus? What's the emergency response plan for your office or job? Then what?

If you have kids in school or daycare, what happens if the school is affected? Do you know what your school's emergency evacuation plan is? Add the information to your PIC (Step #11).

If you or a family member requires dialysis, oncology treatment, or therapy, do you know what the provider's emergency plans are? If you have home care assistance, what are their plans? Ask questions and find out details. Knowing ahead of time will help you plan and deal with the emergency better. Do they have something in writing that you could add to your PIC (Step #11)?

He who fails to plan, plans to fail.

Proverb

What are your top three hazards again? (page 7)

#1: _____

#2: _____

#3: _____

You won't always be at home during a disaster. Where will you meet if you are at work or out shopping? *What-if* the kids are at school or daycare?

These questions and more will help you decide on the designated places you'll meet up at if you can't get home. Consider one outside of your neighborhood and one outside of town if the event impacts the town. Consider the homes of family members, or a public location easy to get to and which might have amenities such as food, warmth or air conditioning, and lodging nearby. Appendix F has additional questions to ask.

Appendix E has a Family Communication Plan form to use. In addition to your designated meeting places, the form has a place to include your contacts for checking-in in Step #15 (Make a Plan — Check-In) and household and other important contact information. Add this form to your PIC (Step #11) after the first tab.

Download a Family Communication Plan at www.dhucks.com/resources-31-smallsteps-emergencies.

Rather than sharing the full communication plan, consider printing business card sized plans with the emergency meeting places and contacts. A blank template is shown in Appendix E and is available for download at www.dhucks.com/resources-31-smallsteps-emergencies.

SUMMARY

Pick ONE action to take today:

- ❑ Decide on a neighborhood meeting location.

- ❑ Determine a meetup location outside of town.

Possible Next Actions:

- ❑ Schedule a game night with the family and play *what-if*.

- ❑ Schedule a date to meet at your spot to get familiar with it. Make it fun!

- ❑ Ask your company or school when the next evacuation drill is and join in with a discussion at home about it.

Resources:

- • Download plans: www.dhucks.com/resources-31-smallsteps-emergencies.

Add Notes Here ⬂

ONE action today

- ❑ Decide on a neighborhood meeting location.

- ❑ Determine a meetup location outside of town.

Make a Plan — Check-In

Happy people plan actions, they don't plan results.

Dennis Wholey

You may not be able to stop your family and friends worrying about you in an emergency, but everyone should understand when and how you'll communicate during a disaster.

In my family, it was understood that if you didn't hear from a person in the first 48 hours, assume everything was fine and they were focused on responding to the situation. Nowadays, if you can't get a response within hours, others are filling up your social media and your phone with "are you all right?" messages.

The best solution is to plan how and when you'll communicate in case of emergency or a disaster. Then tell your friends and family about your plan. Have a conversation about expectations and what's likely and possible.

IDENTIFY TWO EMERGENCY CONTACTS

Choose emergency contacts who don't live with you. Have a local (in town) contact and an out-of-town contact.

Of course, you'll be trying to contact your immediate family to let them know you're okay (or checking on them) when something happens and you're not together. But, you won't always be able to connect. Maybe they're affected by the storm or power outage as well. Decide ahead of time on two emergency contacts outside of your immediate family. Determine who will be your local contact and who will be the out-of-town contact for your household.

You will need to tell family members who aren't in your household who your contact is. That way they can call your contact to see if you've checked-in and are okay. Once they're sure you're safe, they'll relax and won't interrupt your focus on dealing with events. Obviously, that means you've communicated the plan to your contacts and asked for permission to share their information with others.

Your local contact could be a neighbor, a friend who lives in the same area, or a family member in the next town over.

When deciding on a local contact, consider the ways that you'll be able to contact them.

Do they have a standard landline and a Trimline phone that doesn't require power? Then they'll still be able to answer the phone if the power is out. Is their cell phone with a different carrier than yours? If your carrier is down, theirs might be up.

Have an out-of-town contact identified for your household. Sometimes it's easier to get a phone call through if it's long distance and outside of the affected area. Your contact won't be impacted by any power outage or local storm.

All household members should have the names of the identified contacts and their numbers in their cell phones. But you'll need a backup plan in case your cell phone is dead. Carry a business card in your wallet or purse with your contacts' name, number, and whether it will be a phone call only or will they receive texts. Add the Meeting Places from Step #14 (Make a Plan — Meetup). Business card sized forms are available in Appendix E (Family Communication Plan) along with the full Family Communication Plan form to add to your PIC (Step #11).

Remember to text rather than call your contacts during an emergency or disaster. Texts are more likely to get through. Call 911 if it's an emergency. In addition, the details you send in a text can be referred to again and won't depend on a memory under stress.

IN CASE OF EMERGENCY (ICE) CONTACT

You may or may not have heard about adding "ICE" information into your contact list on your cell phone. ICE stands for In Case of Emergency and most EMTs, firefighters, and police know to look in your contacts for ICE if needed. Then again maybe they don't. There are numerous blogs and news articles that take one side or the other on the importance and recognition of ICE contacts. Many emergency responders will check for ICE contacts — if they can get into your mobile phone.

Who's Your Contact?

ICE / #: _____

Local: _____
Home: _____ / Cell: _____
Email: _____ / Social Media: _____

Out-of-Town: _____
Home: _____ / Cell: _____
Email: _____ / Social Media: _____

Where Will You Meet?

Neighborhood: _____
Address: _____

In Town: _____
Address: _____

Out of Town: _____
Address: _____

If there is vital medical information that EMTs and doctors need to have, a medical ID bracelet is more important than an ICE contact in your phone.

If you need a medical ID bracelet but don't already have one — purchasing one may be your ONE action today.

In Case of
Emergency
555-555-5555

If you're in an emergency or disaster, focus on getting to safety and remaining safe. Contact family when it's safe to do so.

For iPhone users, you can add an emergency contact(s) to your Health App. The emergency contact(s) are then available through the "Emergency" function on the lock screen. The EMTs could then press *Medical ID to see your emergency contacts.

For Android users, at time of publication, having an emergency contact accessible from the locked screen depends on the version of the phone. First look for an emergency contact field under "My Information". Some phones may allow you to add emergency contacts directly on the "Emergency Call" screen.

Even simpler is to add contact information to an image and use it as your Lock Screen photo. Or you could get a phone wallet or a card pocket to go on the back of your phone. Carry your In Case of Emergency contact there. Add a card to your wallet with the same information.

USING SOCIAL MEDIA TO COMMUNICATE YOU'RE SAFE

If you're in an emergency or disaster, focus on getting to safety and remaining safe. Contact family when it's safe to do so. During an emergency or disaster, your local lines of communication may be overwhelmed. Stay off communication lines (phone and internet) to allow calls for emergency help to get through and for emergency responders to respond and communicate as needed.

Because social media is a common way to stay in touch these days, it's important to plan how you'll communicate and what you'll say during a disaster or emergency. Think about whether you're going to provide a detailed account, a simple "I'm fine", or snap a selfie to show you're well. Or is social media going to be the last thing you jump on when you're in the middle of things? Whatever your intended response is, let family and friends know ahead of time so they'll be prepared. Letting them know doesn't have to be a formal announcement (though it could be). It could be a casual chat the next time you see an emergency or a disaster in the news. Share what you would do in that situation.

If you've been on Facebook, you may have heard, seen or participated in the Facebook Safety Check. The Safety Check is activated when enough people are posting about an incident. If Facebook determines you're in the affected area you may be prompted to go to Safety Check and let your friends know you're safe or not in the area. You can also invite other friends to mark themselves safe, ask for help, or offer to give help. Take five minutes now and go to www.facebook.com/about/safetycheck. It's a quick overview of Facebook's Safety Check.

Learn about Facebook's Safety Check at www.facebook.com/about/safetycheck.

There is a downside to Facebook's Safety Check. During more localized emergencies, you or a friend may be requested to check in safe when in reality the emergency doesn't affect you. The need to be connected at all times adds stress and can spread fear when it wouldn't otherwise. Share your communication plan with family (and friends) to let them know how and when you'll be in touch.

Remember, when posting to any social media, keep personal information and details to a minimum. You do not want the whole world to know your location or that home has been left empty.

When posting to social media, **keep personal information and details to a minimum.**

ONE action today

- ☐ Identify your out-of-town contact.

- ☐ Add contact name and number(s) to your phones.

- ☐ Add the info to emergency communication plan.

- ☐ Make a hard copy of the contact info and carry it in your backpack, purse, or wallet.

- ☐ Let the contact know.

SUMMARY

Pick ONE action to take today:

- ☐ Identify your out-of-town contact. And tell your family.

- ☐ Add contact name and number(s) to your phones.

- ☐ Add the information to your emergency communication plan.

- ☐ Make a hard copy of the contact information and carry it in your backpack, purse, or wallet.

- ☐ Of course, let the contact know ☺

Possible Next Actions:

- ☐ Add 'ICE' contact(s) to phones.

- ☐ Determine your social media communication plan and share it with family.

- ☐ Create a written Family Communication Plan using the template in Appendix E. You can download the plan template at www.dhucks.com/resources-31-smallsteps-emergencies. Add your meeting places from Step #14 (Make a Plan — Meetup).

- ☐ Create a neighborhood plan and call list to ensure that anyone who needs additional assistance due to age, mobility, or other challenges is taken care of during an emergency. We are stronger together than we are on our own.

Resources:

- Facebook safety check:
  www.facebook.com/about/safetycheck

- Download plans: www.dhucks.com/resources-31-smallsteps-emergencies.

Add Notes Here ↘

16 Microchip Your Pets

Four steps to achievement. Plan purposefully. Prepare prayerfully. Proceed positively. Pursue persistently.

William Arthur Ward

Don't let your animal companions be adopted by some other family after a disaster because no one knew they belonged to you. Microchip and register your pets. If your dog or cat is microchipped, make sure they're registered. If they're registered, make sure your contact information is up-to-date.

WHY IS IT IMPORTANT?

The last thing you want to add to the stress of an emergency or a disaster is losing your pet. But if your dog or cat does run away or gets separated from you, you'll want to get them back when they're found. Of the 15,500 dogs that were rescued after Hurricane Katrina in 2005[5] fewer than 20% were reunited with their families. A microchip and up-to-date registration might have made a difference to the other 12,400+ dogs.

Between August 2007 and March 2008, a study was conducted at 53 animal shelters to find out if microchipping works to reunite pets with their pet parents. The good news is that 73% of the stray dogs that came in went home with their owners. Only 63% of lost cats that came to the shelters were reunited with their families, probably because cats are less likely to wear a collar and tag or be microchipped.

Tags and microchips with your **current contact information** are key to reuniting your family if your pets get separated from you.

For those pets that were microchipped, fewer than 60% were registered. And for those pets that were registered, 35% were not recovered because of incorrect or missing contact information.

WHAT IS IT AND HOW MUCH DOES IT COST?

A microchip is an implantable radio-frequency identification (RFID) device about the size of a grain of rice. It is not a GPS tracker nor does it require batteries. A microchip scanner is used to energize the microchip and read the unique identification number. It should last the life of the pet and rarely migrates from where it is implanted.

A microchip is for all your pets — dogs, cats, birds, reptiles, horses, exotics, even fish and cattle can get microchipped. The AVID Microchip is also used at zoos, aquariums (see it *can* be used on fish), and wildlife.

Implanting the microchip is similar to vaccinating your pet. The microchip is typically injected between the shoulder blades with a syringe. Of the handful of pets, I've had microchipped over the years, none of them noticed the extra shot.

The cost of microchipping your pet varies. Your vet can implant the microchip during your next visit (or schedule one sooner just for microchipping). In addition, your local humane society may offer microchipping at a lower cost during special events or as a routine service.

Registering the microchip with a pet recovery service is usually an additional step. There may be a fee depending on the manufacturer. Registration and up-to-date contact information is vital if you want to be reunited with your lost four-legged friend. The shelter or rescue facility will check for a microchip. But if there's nothing registered or the phone number isn't current, the chances of that reunion drops dramatically.

Make sure when you microchip your pet you take the next step and **register** your pet's microchip.

IF YOU DON'T HAVE YOUR PET MICROCHIPPED, THEN...

1. SCHEDULE an appointment with your vet or look for an event hosted by your local humane society. Either go to their website and look for events or call and ask.

2. MICROCHIP your pets.

3. ASK how the microchip will be registered. Will the vet or shelter register it or do you have to do it? This is the missing step for many owners, myself included. For years I thought my dogs and cats were registered. After all, I'd paid for the microchip, hadn't I? It turns out I was wrong! Yes, my pets were registered in Hawai'i because I had registered with the local humane society

and their LOCAL database. During the move to Pennsylvania, I unknowingly risked the safe return of my dogs and cats because they were not registered in the manufacturer's database or even a universal pet recovery database.

4. REGISTER your pet's microchip and provide your contact information to ensure a safe and timely return of your pet in the event they are lost. For a list of manufacturers and pet recovery systems, keep scrolling to the bottom.

Keep your contact information current.

5. REVIEW and UPDATE your microchip registration annually.

IF YOU ALREADY HAVE YOUR PET MICROCHIPPED, THEN...

1. CONFIRM the microchip is registered. Did you previously register it with a pet recovery service? Check with the service.

    If you don't know or can't remember, use the AAHA Universal Pet Microchip Lookup Tool at www.petmicrochiplookup.org. They will direct you to the service that the microchip number is registered with or to the manufacturer.

2. If the microchip is not registered, REGISTER it with the manufacturer.

Keep your contact information current.

3. If the microchip is registered, CONFIRM contact information is current.

4. ADD an annual REMINDER to your calendar to confirm your pet's microchip is in place and readable. Enter a reminder a year from now or on August 15, which is *Check the Chip Day.* Your local humane society may hold events to check microchips. Or ask your vet to check the next time you take Fido or Fluffy in for shots. In addition, check that the registry has your current contact information.

MICROCHIP MANUFACTURERS — THE LARGEST THREE

911PetChip™ — 911petchip.com

- Pet Recovery Registration Service: FreePetChipRegistry™ www.FreePetChipRegistry.com

- 24/7/365 support

- Will enroll any brand with lifetime registration for free, no annual maintenance fees, no charge for address changes.

- Enroll: online at www.FreePetChipRegistry.com

- Update your contact online at www.FreePetChipRegistry.com.

- Lost Pet: online at www.FreePetChipRegistry.com

- Non-solicitation policy: stated policy that your contact information will not be sold.

- Microchip is pre-registered with the clinic or shelter that implants it. This may help in recovery of your pet if you forget to register.

Avid® — avidid.com

- Pet Recovery Registration Service: PETtrac™ avidid.com/pettrac/enrollment

- 24-hour hotline and support

- Will enroll any brand of microchip with a lifetime enrollment and no annual fees. At the time of publication, enrolling a single pet in the PETtrac Pet Recovery Network cost $19.95 and a package deal of three pets was $49.95. Active duty military personnel pay only $9.95 per pet.

- Enroll: online at avidid.com/pettrac/enrollment or go to avidid.com/pettrac/forms to download the form to register by fax or mail

- Update your contact information at 1-800-336-2843 and pay $6 for the information change.

- Lost Pet: call 1-800-336-2843 if your pet is lost or complete an online report at avidid.com/lost

- Non-solicitation policy: review their privacy policy (avidid.com/privacy-policy). There's no statement that they won't sell your information, but they do post that your personally identifiable information will be used with "qualified third-parties for the purpose of the welfare or recovery of your pet."

Microchip I.D. Solutions Inc — microchipidsolutions.com

- Pet Recovery Registration Service: 1-855-373-8943 or www.microchipidsolutions.com/forms

- Provides lifetime registration at time of implant, no annual maintenance fees, no charge for address changes. Since they don't specifically state registration of any microchip, assume it is for manufacturer's only.

- Enroll: go to www.microchipidsolutions.com/forms to download the form. You can either fax the form or call the number to register your pet's microchip. Details are on the form.

- Update your contact information by calling 1-855-373-8943.

- Lost Pet: call 1-855-373-8943 if your pet is lost.

- Non-solicitation policy: unknown

Though FreePetChipRegistry™ and PETtrac™ will register any brand of microchip, be aware that in the study of the animal shelters, 17.2% of the animals were not reunited because the pet had been registered in a database different from the manufacturer. I don't know how they knew they were registered in a different database but were unable to get them back to their owners, but I don't think it's worth saving $20 dollars to never see your dog or cat again because of that mistake.

PET RECOVERY SERVICES

There are many Pet Recovery Services available. Start with the manufacturer of your microchip. That's probably the first place an animal shelter or vet will search. If you want to register your pet with another service, check out the services that participate with the AAHA Universal Pet Microchip Lookup (www.petmicrochiplookup.org/participating_companies.aspx).

ONE action today

- ❑ Microchip your pet
- ❑ Register your pet's microchip
- ❑ Confirm contact information is current

SUMMARY

Pick ONE action to take today:

- ❑ Microchip your pet
- ❑ Register your pet's microchip
- ❑ Confirm contact information is current

Possible Next Actions:

- ❑ Check the chip each year (August 15, annual vet visit, or check with your local humane society)

Resources:

- ❑ Universal Pet Microchip Lookup Tool at www.petmicrochiplookup.org.
- ❑ Microchip manufacturer: 911petchip.com
    - o Registration: www.FreePetChipRegistry.com
- ❑ Microchip manufacturer: avidid.com
    - o Registration: avidid.com/pettrac/enrollment
- ❑ Microchip manufacturer: microchipidsolutions.com
    - o Registration: www.microchipidsolutions.com/forms

Add Notes Here ↘

Shelter in Place

As you worked your way through these *Small Steps*, you added to your emergency kit, prepared your pets, and planned your communications and meeting places during a disaster. Now it's time to prepare to shelter in place. You may need to take shelter from a tornado, a winter storm, a hurricane, or other hazard. You may need to evacuate the area — I'll cover community shelters in Step #18. Or you may need to stay where you are to avoid the hazards outside — you'll need to *shelter in place*.

Though emergencies don't wait to happen until we get home, this Step will be focused primarily on preparing your home to be your primary shelter if your local authorities announce that you should *shelter in place*. In this step, you will 1) determine whether you'll stay put and shelter in place or evacuate for each of your top three hazards and 2) choose **ONE action to prepare your home** or **ONE item to add to** your emergency kit or shelter.

What are your top three hazards from page 7? Write them in the column to the left. Would you shelter in place for your #1 hazard? Your #2 hazard? What about your #3 hazard? Sheltering in place may not be right for every hazard, such as flooding, a tsunami, or fire, but you want to be prepared if you need to shelter at home.

As you continue reading you'll see many possible next actions to take. Remember, the goal is to be better prepared than you were when you started. Do not be overwhelmed by the list of actions. **Choose ONE** to move forward with. You can return to this step as often as you want to take one more action and then another when you're ready. The focus is on preparing to shelter long before the disaster arrives.

If you ever face a significant disaster, do your best to keep up the spirits of those around you, act flexibly and creatively to help, try to sort rumors from truth, and remember that the decisions you make will have repercussions after the disaster has passed.

Sheri Fink

What are your top three hazards again? (page 7)

#1: _____

#2: _____

#3: _____

Are you likely to stay put and shelter in place?

#1: _____

#2: _____

#3: _____

CHOOSE A ROOM FOR SHELTER

One room may be a good choice for all your hazards, or you may need different locations depending on the situation.

For tornadoes, shelter below ground in a basement room or a storm cellar, or choose a small interior room without windows on the lowest level. Other options may be a closet or interior hallway away from windows, doors, and outside walls. You may have heard somewhere that a bathtub is a safe location during a tornado. If the bathtub is in an interior bathroom with no windows and on the lowest level, then it might give you added protection. You may need to shelter for several hours but not for days.

Hurricanes pose an extreme wind hazard but also have the potential for flooding. That small windowless, interior room or closet may be perfect for the wind, but may not be ideal if there is flooding. Be prepared to move your supplies and shelter to a higher floor (or evacuate).

In choosing your shelter for long-term incidents such as hurricanes, consider the availability of adjoining bathroom facilities, wired phone line capability, and cell phone, television, and radio signal.

GATHER SUPPLIES TO SHELTER FROM ANY HAZARD

For all situations:

❑ The **emergency kit** you've been building (Step #6).

❑ A **whistle** — Place a whistle in your shelter, emergency kit, purse, backpack, car, and on your keychain. If you are trapped by debris, it is easier to indicate your position using your whistle than it is to yell. It saves energy and carries farther. Another option is an air horn. This is an option to add in Step #24 (Extras — Pick ONE).

❑ **Food & Water** — The goal is to have a minimum of two weeks of food and water on hand for sheltering in place.

If you're likely to stay put during an emergency, where in your house will you take shelter?

#1: _____

#2: _____

#3: _____

Steps #21 and #22 will provide details on what you need to know and prepare for when it comes to water (Step #21) and food (Step #22).

❑ **Duct tape** — Though it may not really be the strongest force in the world, it is an extremely adaptable tool. Add one roll to your emergency kit and one roll in your shelter supplies. This is also an option to add in Step #24 (Extras — Pick ONE).

❑ **NOAA Weather Radio** — include a battery-operated or solar/wind-up powered radio in your emergency kit. The NOAA Weather Radio All Hazards (NWR) network broadcasts official Weather Service warnings, watches, forecasts and other hazard information 24 hours a day, 7 days a week. And another option to add in Step #24 (Extras — Pick ONE).

❑ **First aid kit** — Now may be the time to add a first aid kit to your emergency kit or build up your home kit. See Step #5 for a list of items to include.

❑ **Blankets and pillows** — Blankets may be used for warmth during a winter storm, protection from flying debris during a tornado, or a more comfortable bed for an overnight stay in your shelter. If you have space, consider getting a heavy cargo blanket for protection from flying debris in addition to the usual blankets for warmth and comfort.

❑ **Sanitary supplies for pets** — Though you may have sufficient warning to collect items to shelter in place, you may not. Having the following items ready when you bring your animals inside to shelter will make everything easier:

    o   litter and box for cats,

    o   puppy pads or newspapers for dogs,

    o   plastic bags, bleach, paper towels

❑ **Sanitary supplies for people** if there's no bathroom available.

- o 5-gallon bucket
- o Heavy-duty plastic trash bags (use two at a time)
- o Cat litter
- o Snap-on toilet seat and lid made for 5-gallon buckets
- o Toilet paper or moist towelettes
- o Moist towelettes and hand-sanitizer
- o Twist ties or zip ties

ACTIONS TO TAKE FOR ANY HAZARD

Well Before — when there's no emergency or disaster

❑ If you use medical equipment in your home that requires electricity, talk to your doctor or health care provider about how you can prepare for its use during a power outage.

❑ Talk with your insurance agent about your insurance needs.

❑ Continue to prepare your house and your family.

❑ Learn how to safely shut off your utilities. Step #29 (Get Trained / Get Involved).

❑ Have fire extinguishers available and ensure everyone is trained on how to use them.

Before — hours or days before the storm is due to hit your area

❑ Listen to your radio and check your FEMA or National Weather Service (NWS) phone apps for updates.

❑ Fill up your car (Step #2).

❑ Get money from your ATM/bank. Increase your cash on hand.

❑ Charge all phones and electronics.

❑ Charge all batteries for radios, flashlights, medical equipment, etc. And buy more batteries if needed.

❑ Turn your refrigerator and freezers to coldest setting. If power is lost during the storm, in order to maintain the temperature for as long as possible, do not open them unless necessary.

❑ Increase ice production and freeze all reusable ice packs.

❑ Freeze additional bags or bottles of water if you have room. Leave an inch or more of space in the bottle or bag for expansion of the ice.

❑ Fill food-grade containers with drinking water, if you don't already have your emergency water supply. See Step #21 (Water) for details.

❑ Fill all other containers with water for non-potable water needs. See Step #21 (Water) for details.

❑ Unplug all unnecessary appliances.

❑ Get emergency kit and emergency supplies, if not already present.

❑ Review your plans for meeting locations (Step #14), checking-in (Step #15), and evacuating (Steps #18 and #19).

❑ Bring in outside animals if possible.

During — you could be sheltering in place for a couple of hours or several days.

❑ Close and lock doors and windows. Though not routinely mentioned, locking may provide more stability to the window or door during high winds and a tighter seal against outside air.

❑ Continue to listen to your radio for updates and an all-clear announcement. Your FEMA or NWS phone app may provide updates, but it also drains your phone's battery. If there is a power outage, reserve your phone's battery for calls and texts. See Step #3 (Lines of Communication) for other ways to conserve your phone's power.

After — the storm has ended and recovery starts.

❑ Stay safe and aware of your surroundings.

❑ Shut off utilities if necessary and safe to do so.

❑ Begin the recovery process, see Step #30 (Prep for Recovery).

❑ Check on your neighbors.

PREPARATIONS TO MAKE FOR SPECIFIC HAZARDS

Earthquakes

You won't be "sheltering in place" during an earthquake as there is no warning. However, the Federal Emergency Management Agency (FEMA) offers a checklist for homeowners to hunt down and mitigate potential hazards. Consider the following:

❑ Purchase earthquake insurance — call your insurance company.

❑ Secure top-heavy furniture to wall studs with straps.

❑ Secure electronics, fish tanks, heavy objects that can fall, and items hanging on walls (mirrors, pictures, etc.) with flexible nylon straps, closed hooks, adhesives, or earthquake putty.

❑ Remove any items placed above beds or seating areas.

❑ Secure cabinet doors and drawers with child-proof latches to keep them closed and the contents inside.

❑ Secure water heaters, refrigerator, and other appliances with straps or braces — call a contractor.

❑ Brace chimneys — call a contractor.

❑ Use flexible gas line and appliance connections — call a qualified plumber.

❑ Strengthen weak crawlspace walls — call a contractor.

❑ For more information on strengthening new and existing homes, check out FEMA's Homebuilders' Guide to Earthquake-Resistant Design and Construction, www.fema.gov/media-library/assets/documents/6015

❑ During an earthquake:

1. DROP to the ground

2. COVER your head and neck with your arms

   ▪ If you can move safely, crawl for additional cover such as a sturdy table or an interior wall (away from windows).

3. HOLD ON until shaking stops

Floods

Though you're not likely to "shelter in place" during a flood either, here are some actions to take well before a flood threatens your home:

❑ Consider your risk. Are you located in a low-lying area near a river or stream, on the coast, downstream of a dam or levee, or in a flood zone? Maybe you're on a hilltop but there's an underground spring nearby and the risk is rising ground water levels.

❑ Look at the risk differently. If you're in a 100-year floodplain, your risk isn't just every 100 years. There's a one in five chance that a flood will occur in the next 25 years.[6]

❏ Purchase flood insurance — call your insurance company.

❏ Make a plan to get to higher ground. Establish more than one route for evacuation.

❏ Making structural changes to your home in order to reduce the flood risk will require professional help. Check out the FEMA document, *FEMA P-1037, Reducing Flood Risk to Residential Buildings That Cannot Be Elevated (2015)*, www.fema.gov/media-library/assets/documents/109669, for a range of risk reduction measures to consider.

❏ Avoid walking or driving through flood waters. Six inches of moving water can knock you off your feet. A foot of water can sweep your vehicle away.

Hurricanes

Federal Emergency Management Agency (FEMA) offers a checklist for homeowners to avoid hurricane risks that include:

Well Before

❏ Purchase hurricane and/or flood insurance — call your insurance company.

❏ Install hurricane straps or clips to help keep your roof in place and connected to the walls in high winds — call a contractor.

❏ Install and maintain storm shutters or use 5/8-inch thick exterior-grade plywood sheets to cover windows and glass doors — call a contractor.

❏ Reinforce your garage door with heavier brackets to the glider wheel track and by adding hardware across the back of the door, or replace it with a door that is approved for both wind pressure and impact protection — call your garage door expert.

❑ Remove trees that could fall on your home. If you're planting trees, keep in mind what its full-grown height will be and plant it that far away from your house plus a little more.

❑ FEMA also has guidance documents for building a residential safe room to protect you from extreme windstorms (hurricanes and tornadoes) so you can shelter in place.

Before

❑ Anchor or remove potential windborne objects like trash cans, yard furniture, barbecue grills, playground equipment, and more. Anchor storage sheds.

❑ Close the storm shutters or put up the plywood sheets over windows and glass doors.

❑ Tape glass windows on the inside with large Xs to reduce shattering. This lessens the hazard of flying glass debris. Use shipping tape if possible. Duct tape will work but may be difficult to remove.

❑ Draw curtains and blinds. Again, this reduces the hazard of flying debris.

❑ Go Low! If you have the option of multiple shelters in your home, go low. However, if your home is in a flood zone and might be flooded during a hurricane, thunderstorm or other severe weather event, you don't want to be trapped by storm waters.

<u>Tornadoes</u>

You will need to take shelter during a tornado, though it may only be for a short period of time. In addition to the structure reinforcements for hurricane preparedness above, consider the following actions for tornadoes:

Well Before

- ❑ If you don't have a safe room built to FEMA criteria to shelter in, the next best choice is a small, windowless, interior room on the lowest level.

- ❑ If you live or work in a mobile home, identify another nearby shelter or structure that can withstand the high winds.

During

- ❑ While sheltering, use a sturdy table and blankets, pillows or a heavy coat to provide additional protection.

- ❑ Cover your head and neck with your arms.

Winter Storms
(snowstorms and extreme cold)

Snowstorms and extreme cold can keep you homebound for days, and power outages are always a concern. Watch or listen for the weather reports in your area and take precautions before the storm hits.

- ❑ Ensure your home is well insulated BEFORE winter.

- ❑ Add weather stripping around doors and windows. Identify other areas that may need additional TEMPORARY insulation or coverage (with a blanket or plastic sheeting) such as pet doors, dryer vents, or even rooms.

- ❑ Know how to shut off the water in case of a burst pipe.

- ❑ Keep the pipes from freezing by turning the water on at a slow run or trickle (more than just a drip).

- ❑ Determine how you can stay warm if the power goes out. Your gas furnace probably requires electricity, so be prepared with:

- ○ Additional blankets, sleeping bags, and warm winter coats.

- ○ If you have a wood-burning stove or fireplace, stock plenty of firewood.

- ○ If you have a gas fireplace, determine if yours uses a 'standing pilot' or an 'intermittent pilot'. The standing pilot is always lit and doesn't require electricity but the intermittent pilot does. Some of the energy saving gas fireplaces have a battery back-up. Verify your system before the storm hits.

❑ Do NOT use a gasoline generator, or a propane, natural gas, wood or charcoal burning grill, stove, or other device inside. They generate carbon monoxide and are fire hazards. A wood-burning stove or fireplace or a gas fireplace installed by a professional is exempt because proper ventilation has been installed and is set-up to code.

❑ Install carbon monoxide monitors in central locations on every level and outside of sleeping areas. If your monitors are hard wired, remember to change out the batteries at least annually to ensure the monitors continue to work during a power outage.

❑ Have fire extinguishers available and ensure everyone is trained on how to use them.

❑ Keep your exhaust vents free and clear of snow. This includes furnace, hot water heater, and other appliances.

Cold or flu
(a disaster is bad enough but what if you're sick too)

❑ Stock your pantry with at least a two-week supply of food.

❑ Have any nonprescription drugs and other health supplies on hand. Don't wait to get sick to buy them. Include:

- o pain relievers,
- o stomach remedies,
- o cough and cold medicines,
- o fluids with electrolytes, and
- o vitamins.

❑ Have other items you use during an illness, including

- o hand soap,
- o facial tissues,
- o hand-sanitizer, at least 60% alcohol,
- o latex gloves, and
- o disposable facemask.

❑ Practice good personal health habits NOW

- o Stay home when you're sick.
- o Stay home at least another 24 hours after you no longer have a fever (without the use of meds).
- o Cover your coughs and sneezes with a tissue or your sleeve.
- o Wash your hands, front and back and under your nails, with soap and water for at least 20 seconds. Hum the 'happy birthday song' twice.
- o Clean frequently touched surfaces and objects. These can include faucet handles, door knobs, stair rails, remote controls, etc.

There are a lot of possible actions to take in this step, but don't let that stop you from taking action on just ONE thing. Choose to do what you can today. Then when you're ready you can look at taking another action.

SUMMARY

Pick ONE action to take today:

- ❑ Choose a room for shelter based on your top three hazards.

- ❑ Choose ONE item to add to your emergency kit or shelter.

- ❑ Choose ONE action to prepare your home for your #1 hazard.

Possible Next Actions:

- ❑ Plan and prepare to shelter in place at work.

- ❑ Create a commuter emergency plan for the commute between home and work, school or shopping.

- ❑ Plan and prepare for kids to shelter in place at school. Find out what your schools' plans are and how they practice.

- ❑ Plan and prepare to shelter in your vehicle. Get an emergency kit for the car. NOTE: a vehicle should be a last resort for sheltering in place. It can be a dangerous place during some hazards such as high wind events and floods. Go to www.ready.gov/tornadoes to learn more about using a vehicle as shelter in a tornado.

- ❑ When traveling, make a habit of identifying where you might shelter in an emergency. Some airports have tornado shelters. Start a 'what-if' conversation with your hotel staff about local hazards and plans.

ONE action today

- ❑ Choose a room to shelter in place.

- ❑ Choose ONE item to add to your emergency kit or shelter.

- ❑ Choose ONE action to prepare your home.

Resources:

- Earthquakes:
    - FEMA, *Earthquake Home Hazard Hunt*, bit.ly/2rAnRrQ
    - FEMA 232, *Homebuilders' Guide to Earthquake-Resistant Design and Construction (2006)*, bit.ly/2vpJ6hZ
    - Shake Out™, www.shakeout.org

- Flooding: www.fema.gov/media-library/assets/documents/109669

- Hurricanes: www.fema.gov/pdf/media/factsheets/2011/avoiding_hurricane_damage.pdf

- Tornadoes: www.ready.gov/tornadoes

- Building a safe room:
    - www.fema.gov/safe-rooms
    - www.fema.gov/residential-safe-rooms
    - www.fema.gov/fema-p-320-taking-shelter-storm-building-safe-room-your-home-or-small-business

- Commuter emergency plan: www.fema.gov/media-library-data/1390856235302-ff6e316df62851d5a5afe834b4fcd53c/Commuter_Emergency_Plan_v7_508.pdf

- Individuals with Disabilities: www.ready.gov/individuals-access-functional-needs

Add Notes Here ⬂

Community Shelter

If you can't shelter in place, don't have friends and family to shelter with, or enough room on a credit card to cover a hotel stay, a community shelter may be your only option in a disaster. You need to be prepared to make the shelter stay as easy and comfortable as possible.

First, take your emergency kit, your PIC and all the other supplies on your Grab & Go checklist. The following should already be on your checklist, but if not, add them to it.

Bring your **pillow and a blanket or sleeping bag**. Red Cross and other shelters *may* have cots but they may not supply the bedding. You will need sleep and having your own pillow is comforting. You'll need something to soften the cot (or floor) and to keep you warm.

Pack **clothes or pajamas to sleep in** which you won't mind 500 of your new closest acquaintances seeing you in. A t-shirt and yoga pants, comfortable shorts, or light sweats might be ideal. Think of lounging comfort.

Change of **clothes and clean underwear**. Again, as stated in Step #8 (Build a Kit — Clothes and Hygiene), it's amazing what clean underwear can do for your confidence and comfort. You won't be packing for a vacation, but you will pack for an extended stay. But remember, community shelters can be crowded; you won't have room for multiple luggage pieces.

If you have time and space to add in stadium chairs or folding chairs, do it. Some shelters may have only bleachers or the floor to sit on. At the same time, you may not have much room. Shelters are intended to give you shelter; they won't give you a lot of privacy or space.

During an emergency there are two types of community shelters, evacuation and congregate care. Evacuation shelters are

... her resilient resourcefulness represents the ordinary response in many disasters. In them, strangers become friends and collaborators, goods are shared freely, people improvise new roles for themselves.

Rebecca Solnit
A Paradise Built in Hell

You won't have much privacy or space in a shelter. Bring pillows and sleeping bags, clothes to sleep in, and a change of clothes. Remember to bring your medication and medical devices you need.

intended to be short-term safe places to ride out the storm until it's safe for you to return home and get back to daily life. Congregate care shelters provide housing needs for individuals in a community displaced by a disaster. It is not a long-term solution but may be needed for several weeks.

As you can imagine, the needs, supplies, and services for a short-term evacuation shelter will be more bare-bones then for a congregate care shelter which, over time, may add additional capacity. A limiting factor is the number of volunteers available to open and staff shelters. Consider volunteering and get the training through your local Red Cross chapter or other sheltering organization in Step #29 (Get Trained / Get Involved).

There may not be amenities to wash your clothes. Consider adding travel-size laundry soap to your emergency kit to do basic laundry in the sink.

Food may be provided depending on how long the shelter will be opened for. For evacuation shelters, don't count on meals being provided. Mass feeding becomes a priority for the congregate care shelters. Your snacks and meals from your emergency kit will provide a familiar taste but may not be necessary. Keep in mind that you may be required to eat only in the designated eating areas to keep the sleeping/living areas as clean as possible.

Once the shelter is set up and filled, there may be jobs and tasks you can do to assist shelter staff and your fellow residents. Think of these things as opportunities to help and to stave off boredom. Too much free time can make the time go slowly and allows too much time to worry and stress.

Plan to stay active and engaged by helping out at the shelter, finding space to walk or exercise, and bring low-tech entertainment, such as a book, paper puzzles, etc.

Stay active. Find a safe path to walk inside or outside and get up and walk it several times a day. Even if it is just around the outside of the living quarters, get your steps in. Find space to do stretches or arm lifts. Do what you can to stay active and healthy. Again, this helps the time go by and also keeps your spirits up.

If you've added a book, games, or puzzles to your emergency kit they will help to pass the time. Your shelter may have electricity but it may not. It may run off generator power to allow people to recharge essential electronics such as phones, motorized wheel chair batteries, oxygen concentrators, etc. You won't be able to recharge your non-essential electronics. Have a paper copy of games, puzzles and books just in case. The portable power pack from Step #3 may be enough to recharge your mobile device a few times. When you finish your book, you can exchange books with other residents.

Under the American with Disabilities Act, ADA, shelters are required to allow service animals remain with the individual served, but you will be required to take care and maintain control of the animal. You will need to provide food, water, medical and hygiene needs for your service animal.

If you have a service animal, you will be responsible for all its needs. Plan for food, water, and hygiene needs in Step #9.

Pets may or may not be allowed in or near the shelter, so be prepared. Preparing to take care of your animals and pets is next in Step #19 (Plan for Your Animals) and Step #20 (Provide a Safe Cave for Your Pets —Get a Kennel for Each).

SUMMARY

Pick ONE action to take today:

- ❑ Create or update your Grab & Go checklist. This list can double as your vacation or camping packing list. Test it out and update when you get back each time.

- ❑ Add books, games, and puzzles to your emergency kit. Use physical products and not just apps on your phone.

Possible Next Actions:

- ❑ Try out your portable power supply to make sure you know how it works. Purchase one if you haven't already.

- ❑ Add a power strip to your emergency kit. This allows more than one person to charge their devices at a time and is very handy at a shelter.

Add Notes Here ⬂

ONE action today

- ❑ Create or update your Grab & Go checklist.

- ❑ Add physical books, games, and puzzles to your emergency kit.

19 Shelter for Your Animals

As a society, we have improved the way we handle evacuating pets in an emergency. With Hurricane Katrina in 2005, pets were left behind. According to the Louisiana SPCA, 250,000 animals (dogs, cats, horses, guinea pigs, and more) were abandoned during the evacuation before Hurricane Katrina[7]. Of the 15,500 dogs rescued following the disaster, only a third of them, or about 5,000 dogs, were reunited with their families.

With Hurricane Harvey in 2017, both pets and people were evacuated. Many pets were welcomed into shelters or the shelters provided other options. But not every shelter or community is prepared to house and feed pets as well as people, so you will need to plan for your animals too.

Contact your local American Red Cross and ask what their procedure is for pets. Contact your local humane society and find out their procedures. If you don't like the answers, see if there is something you can do to help the volunteer organizations become pet friendly during an emergency.

And be prepared to shelter in place if it's safe. Consider if you can build a safe room for your house so that you may not have to evacuate in all instances.

In Hawai'i, we chose to shelter in place because we were outside the flood zone, our home had a safe room, and there was limited shelter availability for our animals. Local and state governments were working with American Red Cross to allow animals in a separate part of the shelter facilities, and the local humane society was working on plans to take in pets. The issue was that part of the plan required euthanizing any shelter animals awaiting adoption to open up the limited space for pets of evacuees.

During Hurricane Harvey in 2017, nearby shelters outside of the affected areas began transporting shelter animals to shelters

Planning is bringing the future into the present so that you can do something about it now.

Alan Lakein

Learn about your local sheltering capacity.

farther away so that the local animal shelters had capacity to accommodate both evacuated pets and stray animals.

Various agencies across the country continue to talk and plan for emergency responses which include pets and other animals. The plans and procedures continue to improve, but it will take time.

Keep in mind that if you have an exotic pet, such as a snake, lizard, pig, chicken, cougar, etc., they may not be accepted at a public shelter. You will need to ensure your plans take that into account in Step #18 (Community Shelter). And I'm serious about the cougar. In my neighborhood in Montana (yes, I've lived in Montana also) we had restrictions on what animals could be kept as pets. Rabbits, alligators, and cougars were all prohibited. I always wondered what circumstances got each animal listed.

Find out now if your family or friends will take you and your pet if you need to evacuate.

Continue preparing today by talking with family members, friends, and relatives about *what-if* you had to evacuate your pets in case of a house fire or other focused disaster. *What-if* the disaster affected your community? Where could you and your pets go? What-if you had to evacuate the region? Have the conversation now and establish your plans.

Keep vaccinations updated so that if you do shelter Fluffy and Fido with other animals they have the best chance of staying healthy. In addition to rabies, check with your veterinarian about other recommended vaccinations. Routine vaccinations may protect against parvovirus, hepatitis, leptospirosis and distemper for dogs. For cats, again in addition to rabies, recommended vaccinations may include feline distemper and feline leukemia. Ask your vet about vaccinations required for boarding your animal. You may have no plans to board but, then again, you don't intend to experience an emergency or disaster either.

SUMMARY

Pick ONE action to take today:

ONE action today

❑ Identify where you and your pets might shelter.

❑ Update your pet's vaccinations

❑ Identify where you, your family and your pets might shelter if you need to evacuate. Will it be with friends and family? Or will you need to find alternative shelter?

❑ Update your pet's vaccinations. Add shots for boarding.

Possible Next Actions:

❑ Continue to build your pet's emergency supplies (Step #9).

❑ Get your pet comfortable with traveling in the car. Take them on rides to dog parks, walks, doggie day care or anywhere that isn't the vet.

❑ Investigate sheltering options for you and your pet in a 100-mile radius. Print a list and include it in your PIC and pet's emergency supply kit. Consider:

  o Family and friends,

  o Hotels that allow household pet(s),

  o Boarding kennels,

  o Animal shelters and humane societies,

  o Veterinary offices with boarding facilities,

  o Grooming shops, and

  o Approved areas at fairgrounds or parks.

Add Notes Here ↘

Provide a Safe Cave for Your Pets — Get a Kennel for Each

Always focus on how far you've come, not how far you have to go.

Unknown

IATA's Traveler's Pet Corner has guidance on sizing your kennel for your pet.

If you don't already have a kennel for each of your cats or dogs, get one. Begin kennel training now. The best time to kennel train your pets is when they're puppies or kittens, but the next best time is today (or the day you bring the kennel home). Help your pets learn that a kennel is a safe cave for them to curl up in. Never use the kennel as a punishment because you'll want them to feel comfortable and safe there.

As mentioned in Step#13, get the sturdiest kennel you can afford. The IATA (International Air Transportation Association) approved kennels are intended to safely fly your pet from one location to another and they are ideal for kennels in emergencies even if you aren't flying. However, if you *are* evacuating on an airplane, you'll be ready. Each brand will have instructions for sizing, but keep in mind that the kennel should be tall enough for your pet to stand comfortably and long and wide enough for them to turn around. For cats, you'll want the kennel to be big enough to accommodate a litter pan.

Introduce your pet to the kennel before it's an emergency by first feeding them in front of the kennel. Over time, move the food into the kennel, then farther back and eventually all the way back so that your pet is fully inside the kennel. Give them snacks and treats only in the kennels. Then when they're comfortable, close the kennel for a minute or two. Continue the process, keeping them in the kennel for longer periods. If at any time they become skittish or scared, return to a previous step and begin again. Don't think of this as a waste of time, think of this as time you get to play with your dog or cat. The next time I get a kitten, the kennel will be a part of the normal cat jungle gym, and for a puppy it will be a safe sleeping den.

Whether you have a kennel or not, at the first sign of an emergency bring your pets indoors, if possible, especially when there is a chance of an evacuation. This will ensure that they're easily accessible at a moment's notice. Animals may bolt and run away from you and their home in an emergency.

Label each kennel with your pet's name, photo, any special feeding and care instructions, including medications, and the name and phone number of your veterinarian. Make sure **your** name, phone number and other contact information is on the label. Add the name and information for an emergency contact if you can't be reached. You'll need all this if you have to evacuate, even if you can't take your pet with you.

Once you have a kennel, continue to plan ahead. Talk with friends, family, animal shelters, community emergency management organizations, and boarding facilities about where your pets can go in a disaster when you have to evacuate. Will it be with you in a shelter or will you need to evacuate without your pets? Does your local animal shelter have options that can help?

If you must evacuate without your pets and don't have a safer alternative, confine them to a safe place indoors. Keep dogs separated from cats and smaller animals separated from both. They might usually get along fine, but in times of stress, separation keeps each species safer. Allow them to roam freely inside the rooms you've assigned them with plenty of water and food.

If you've had to leave your pets behind at your home, create a notice in large print, with a marker or print a sign that will let emergency personnel know what pets are inside and where they are. Add your phone number or your alternate contact number to this sign. Then place it on your door or in the front window. Make additional signs and place each in a visible location at entry points.

If you can't evacuate your pets, place a sign (large print) on your front door or window to let responders know animals are inside.

ONE action today

- [ ] Get a kennel for each pet.

- [ ] Work with your pet to make it a safe, relaxing place.

SUMMARY

Pick ONE action to take today:

- [ ] Get a kennel for each pet.

- [ ] Work with your pet to make it a safe, relaxing place.

Possible Next Actions:

- [ ] If your pets don't use their kennels every day, bring them out every few months to reintroduce them.

- [ ] Discuss *what-if* scenarios for your pets.

Resources:

- Dimensions for container: www.iata.org/whatwedo /cargo/live-animals/pets/Pages/index.aspx

Add Notes Here ↘

Water

You need clean, safe drinking water. Plan for 1 gallon per person per day. Remember to add a gallon per pet per day as well.

A gallon per person (or pet) may exceed the actual needs of a typical active and healthy person or your teacup chihuahua, but it also allows for sanitation needs. A normally active person needs almost 3/4 of a gallon of fluid every day which can come from water, other non-alcoholic beverages, and food.

Needs may vary with age, health, exertion, diet, and climate. Children, pregnant women, nursing mothers and those who are sick may need more than a gallon a day. You may need more water in warm weather and even more in very hot weather. For pets, as mentioned in Step #9 (Prepare your Pets) you may only need one cup for your six-pound cat or a half gallon per day for your sixty-pound pooch.

Safe water isn't just for drinking. You need water free of contaminants — microbes, solids, and chemicals — to wash dishes and toys. You need safe water to bathe in, to cook with, to brush your teeth with, and you need safe water for ice. You need clean, safe water to wash flood-impacted food packages (see Appendix L for more information).

BEGIN WITH A 3-DAY SUPPLY OF SAFE DRINKING WATER

If you purchase cases of bottled water you will need eight 16-fluid ounce (fl oz) bottles per person per day. A case of bottled water normally contains 24 bottles which would give you enough water for one person for three days. One case per person is a good start. Keep the bottled water sealed and stored in a cool, dark, dry place, away from non-food items such as gasoline, paint, solvents, and cleaning supplies because the plastic is permeable.

Taking a long-term view doesn't require brilliance, but it does require dedication.

Bill Gates

Keep the bottled water sealed and stored in a cool, dark, dry place away from chemicals and solvents.

Guidance for expiration dates on bottled water gets confusing. Ready.gov states *"Water that has* **not** *been commercially bottled should be replaced every six months."* There's no mention of an expiration date. The CDC, on the other hand, directs you to observe the expiration date for the water you buy. Some preparedness blogs may say store-bought bottled water is fine after its expiration date. See Appendix I for more on expiration dates.

My answer to the expiration question is to rotate your supplies. If you drink bottled water, then "shop" from your emergency stash and put the bottled water on your grocery list to restock. If you don't normally drink bottled water, look for opportunities like family picnics or community events to use your aging cases and replace with newer ones.

If you've chosen to fill your own food-grade containers with water, replace and refill at least every six months to maintain a fresh supply.

If you created your emergency kit to hold three days' worth of supplies, lugging around 3 gallons of water per person could be a challenge. Instead, you could purchase a small backpacking or personal water filter and stock three to six bottles of water in your emergency kit. Will it be enough water? Maybe not, but it's portable and continue to work for you after the first three days.

MORE WAYS TO STOCK UP ON WATER

Make your water do double duty. Freeze partially empty bottles of water and use them to keep your food cold until they melt and give you clean, safe drinking water.

Rather than just store bottles of water on the shelf or in the corner, you can have some of your water do double duty by freezing partially empty bottles of water and then using the "ice" to keep your foods frozen in your freezer or cool in your cooler. As the ice melts, you have drinkable water. Leave at least an inch of space to allow for expansion.

You can also purchase water containers (carboys, jerry cans, bottles) in 5-gallon or larger sizes to fill up when you have notice to prepare for a storm. Some things to think about in purchasing are: How much space will it take up when not in use? Do you have that space? How easy will it be to keep clean between uses?

Also consider how easy it will be for you to lift and carry. Five gallons of water is heavy. Adding a food-grade siphon or pump to get to the water without lifting the container may be useful or absolutely necessary for you.

Whatever containers you get should be food-grade and not used for anything other than water.

Refer to Step #22 (Choose Your Food) when stocking your food supplies. Choose foods that are lower in salt, higher in moisture and may even come with added water. Your hydration needs don't have to be filled only from water. Your food should also contain some of the necessary fluid to remain hydrated. But not everything liquid will help you hydrate. Alcoholic beverages are dehydrating, and your body does not build up a tolerance. You may also see notices to avoid caffeinated beverages. Evidence shows that caffeine-containing beverages are no more dehydrating than other non-alcoholic beverages when taken in normal serving sizes.[8]

Another source of hydration: your food. Choose foods low in salt and higher in moisture.

The amount of bottled or packaged water you stock will depend both on the space you have available and how many days you're preparing for, along with how much warning you have.

STOCKING MORE THAN THE 3-DAY SUPPLY OF WATER

As we've seen in recent disasters, communities may be without running water and electricity for more than three days.

Hurricane Maria hit Puerto Rico and the U.S. Virgin Islands on September 19, 2017. Ten days after the hurricane, over 50% of Puerto Rico residents were still without running water[9].

Hurricane Sandy hit the East Coast of the United States on October 29, 2012. It took 13 days for New York utilities to restore power to at least 95 percent of their customers. It took New Jersey utilities 11 days and West Virginia 10 days to reach 95 percent coverage[10].

The Hawai'i Emergency Management Agency now recommends Hawai'i residents gather sufficient emergency supplies to last for 14 days rather than the previously recommended 7 days.[11]

You might not have the space to store more than a 3-day supply of water. You might be flooded out and can't evacuate with your supplies. What can you do? You could collect water ahead of a disaster if you have warning. You could get the supplies to filter and treat any water that is available.

COLLECTING WATER JUST BEFORE

Fill all food-grade water containers (carboys, jerry cans, bottles, jugs). This will be your primary source of potable water that you won't need to treat.

If you know a storm is coming:
- fill all food-grade water containers
- increase ice production
- fill bathtubs, sinks, washing machine and other containers

If you have warning of a storm, increase your ice production. Either set your freezer to automatically make ice more quickly or turn your freezer temperature down as cold as you can make it and make more ice cubes manually. Add more bottles of water (with an inch or more of space for expansion) to the freezer. Even reclosable freezer bags partially filled with water will provide safe drinking water and will also help to keep your food cold. Double bag and remember to label the contents.

If you're sheltering in place, you should also fill your bathtubs, sinks, washing machine, and other containers with water. You'll be able to use this water for toilets if the water is disrupted. Be aware that the stoppers in your sink and bathtub won't hold the water forever. The water will slowly drain. There are bladders built for your bathtub which can hold approximately 100 gallons of water. Get a food-grade siphon or hand pump to go with it.

TREATING THE WATER

After a disaster, the water from your tap (if it's running) may not be safe to drink. You will need to treat it before you use it (drinking, cooking, personal hygiene, or cleaning). Follow the directions and guidelines given by your water company and health officials. You may need to treat the water for possible contaminants such as bacteria, viruses, chemicals, or heavy metals.

Check out Appendix H — Safe Drinking Water

Refer to Appendix H for information on disinfecting or treating your water for microbes along with what to look for in a filtration system if you purchase one.

SUMMARY

Pick ONE action to take today:

- ❑ Decide how much water you will store.

- ❑ Clear space for your emergency water supply.

- ❑ Buy a case of bottled water per person (and pet) in household.

- ❑ Get food-grade water containers for collecting water.

- ❑ Freeze several bottles of water (leaving an inch or more of space for expansion).

Possible Next Actions:

- ❑ Buy unscented liquid household bleach (5-6% or 8.25% of sodium hypochlorite with nothing else added) for disinfecting the water and cleaning.

- ❑ Purchase a water filtration system, whether personal size or for the household, that doesn't require power.

- ❑ Try out your water filter. Don't just buy it and put it on a shelf. Put it together, run water through it. Test it out. Don't wait for an emergency to figure out how it works.

Resources:

- Water: www.ready.gov/water

- Water: www.cdc.gov/healthywater/emergency/drinking/creating-storing-emergency-water-supply.html

- See Appendix H —Safe Drinking Water for more details.

Add Notes Here ➘

ONE action today

- ❑ Decide how much water you will store.

- ❑ Clear space for your emergency water supply.

- ❑ Buy a case of bottled water per person (and pet) in household.

- ❑ Get food-grade water containers for collecting water.

- ❑ Freeze several bottles of water (leaving an inch or more of space

Choose Your Food

*To keep a lamp burning
we have to keep putting
oil in it.*

Mother Teresa

Whether you're planning to use your regular food pantry as your emergency supply or stocking your disaster preparedness kit with packaged meals and foods that are ready to eat, you'll want to choose your food carefully. If you're only focusing on a 3-day supply of food, then almost anything will work, but if you're planning for three weeks, a month, or even a year, you'll need to have nutritious meals to keep you going while you recover from the disaster. Don't just buy a box of Meals Ready to Eat (MREs) or a kit from a survivalist website without looking at a few key factors.

KEY FACTORS TO CONSIDER:

Shelf life — though some commercially available emergency and camping foods have a listed shelf life of thirty years, the U.S. military's guide is three years at 80°F. As the temperature increases, the shelf life decreases.

Shelf life is not necessarily the "best-by" date that we routinely see on food in the supermarket. Shelf life is how long the product is fit to use or consume. That "best-by" date means that the food is at its best quality, not that it's expired, though we often say "expiration date". See Appendix I for best-by-date info.

An extended shelf life may not be necessary if you rotate your emergency supplies. If you do use your emergency supplies as your backup pantry, remember to re-stock routinely.

Look at the nutrition
label on your food.
Limit your salt intake.

Salt content — salt is commonly added to canned and packaged foods (whether emergency supplies or regular everyday items) to enhance taste. But salt increases your need for water, and in an emergency, water may be limited. Look at the nutrition label of emergency food supplies. How much salt does it have? An easy way to evaluate is look at the serving size of the can or pouch. Then look at the Daily Percent of salt. Is it a reasonable serving size for the packet?

Nutrient content — look for protein (you want some) and fat (you want some but not a lot) including the type of fat. Look at the salt as mentioned above. Again, if it's a 3-day supply, then the nutrition content may not be critical, but it will be if you're preparing for weeks or months.

Serving size for each packet — you've seen the soup cans that have 2.5 servings in them and you know you eat more than one serving. The same will occur with your emergency meals. You will want to have a realistic volume of food to help feel satisfied, but you also have to consider the space that the food takes up. Also look at whether the emergency food is packed for individual meal use or all 30 days in one bag. Does the size and package make sense for you and your family during an emergency?

Water requirement — many of the emergency foods require water. If it requires a cup of water per package, will you have enough safe water available? And how will you heat the water?

Before you rush out and purchase packages of emergency foods, plan to prepare your everyday pantry as your first line of emergency food. Instead of waiting to shop when the pantry is bare, create a checklist of staples to always have on hand and some backups.

Consider canned meats, soups, fruits, and vegetables that are moist and come in liquids. Check out the salt though. Many canned vegetables and meat are high in salt. Limit the salt in your emergency foods. You may need to watch your salt intake or want to limit foods that make you thirsty. Sorry, SPAM® may be a handy choice but it's high in salt and fat. Choose packaged tuna, chicken or salmon which generally have half or a third of the salt in SPAM®. Stock up on fruits and vegetables. Canned fruits (in fruit juice not syrup, of course) and veggies are a great way of ensuring that even in a disaster you can get your servings in. Remember a can opener, too — one that's not electric!

Find the balance between comfort and healthy in your emergency food stash. Stock your emergency kit with some treats, and remember to read the nutrition label.

Start your emergency preparations in your food pantry. Keep your pantry stocked with your basic necessities at all times.

Let your emergency stash do double duty. As part of your car's emergency kit, keep healthier foods stashed in the car. It will be there for emergencies and a healthier option before you go shopping or if you're running late.

SUMMARY

Pick ONE action to take today:

❑ Create a checklist of staples to always have on hand.

❑ Read the label and directions before purchasing packaged emergency foods.

❑ Add a manual can opener to your emergency kit. Buy one that is easy to use. Ensure everyone can operate it.

❑ Add a 3-day supply of portable, easy- or no-cook foods to your emergency kit.

Possible Next Actions:

❑ Go for seven days — once you have three days' worth of portable, easy- or no-cook foods, add four more days. Do you want more canned meat, fruit, and veggies, or shelf-stable milk, soup, crackers, granola, trail mix, etc.?

❑ Stock your pantry for 2- to 3-weeks' worth of meals. It doesn't have to be no-cook foods. It can be your usual items that you consume, but now there's no last-minute shopping needs.

❑ Alternative cooking methods — Look at other cooking appliances you have, such as your outdoor grill or your camp stove (use both outside). Try a solar oven. You can purchase them online or find instructions to make your own.

Add Notes Here ↘

ONE action today

❑ Create a checklist of staples to have on hand.

❑ Read the label and directions of packaged emergency foods.

❑ Add a manual can opener and know how to use it.

❑ Add three days' worth of portable, easy- or no-cook foods to your emergency kit.

Build Your Emergency Stash from What You Have

Let your emergency stash do double duty. Choose items for your emergency supplies that can also be used for everyday needs. Or think of what you already have that you can use during an emergency.

Camping gear is the first thing that comes to mind. If you routinely camp, or once upon a time bought gear to go camping, pull it out, check it over, and store it near your emergency preparedness kit. If you can't store it nearby, at least gather all your camping gear in one easy to access location for a quick grab and go if necessary. Some items used for camping that might come in handy for emergencies are:

- ❑ Backpacks

- ❑ Cookware

- ❑ Cooler and blue ice packs

- ❑ Cups

- ❑ Lighting — Headlamps, lanterns, and flashlights.

- ❑ Shelter (tents or tarps),

- ❑ Sleeping bags

- ❑ Sleeping pads

- ❑ Stove

- ❑ Utensils

- ❑ Water filter

- ❑ Water bottles

- ❑ What else would you add to this list?

Dear Optimist, Pessimist, and Realist,

While you guys were busy arguing about the glass of water, I drank it.

Sincerely,
The Opportunist

Facebook post from
Laugh It's Free

If you grill (or at least own one), add this to your list of resources. In case of a power outage, you can use your grill (outside), even in the middle of winter, to boil water and cook a hot meal. Make it a habit to check your propane or charcoal after each summer barbeque and before you put it away for the winter. Restock if it's low. Your picnic items may also be useful during an emergency.

A cooler for camping or picnics will definitely be useful in an emergency. In fact, you may already have used your cooler when your refrigerator broke down and you needed to store your food until it was fixed or the new one arrived. Your cooler is an emergency resource if the power goes out or if you have to evacuate.

If you don't have a cooler, then today's step could be buying one.

In addition to the usual questions to consider when purchasing a cooler (cost, capacity, and performance), consider this:

- Will the cooler fit in the trunk of your car? If the people and animals go up front, will you be able to get the cooler in the back?

- Will the cooler require two people to carry?

- Can **you** carry it?

Consider a medium-sized cooler on wheels. Your emergency food supply will have some important staples, but it won't include everything in your fridge. Look at Appendix J and Appendix K to find which food items can safely be used if you run out of ice or blue ice.

Speaking of refrigeration and food, if there is a power outage but no emergency which requires evacuation, don't open the refrigerator or freezer. The refrigerator should maintain a safe temperature for up to 4 hours. A full freezer (unopened) should maintain temperature for 48 hours and a half full freezer for 24 hours. If you have room BEFORE the emergency, freeze a jug or two of water (remember to save room for expansion). This will increase the time your freezer will keep your foods cold, act as

If the power goes out, keep the refrigerator and freezer closed.

an ice pack in your cooler if needed, and provide fresh, safe drinking water as it melts.

Yet another everyday stash that can do double duty in an emergency is your car's first aid kit. Did you put one in every car in Step #5? Anything to add to it?

SUMMARY

Pick ONE action to take today:

❑ Pull out and check your camping gear. Store it together in an easy access location.

❑ Buy a cooler that you can manage by yourself.

❑ Fill your propane bottle or get another bag of charcoal for your grill.

❑ Freeze a jug or several bottles of water.

❑ Restock your car's first aid kit and food stash.

❑ Choose another action that will let your emergency stash do double duty.

Possible Next Actions:

❑ Build a car emergency kit, see Appendix N. Keep it stocked with healthier foods. It will be there for emergencies and is an option before you go shopping or if you're running late and need some energy.

Resources:

• Coolers: www.outdoorgearlab.com/topics/camping-and-hiking/best-cooler/buying-advice

Add Notes Here ⬎

ONE action today

❑ Check your camping gear. Store it together in an easy access location.

❑ Buy a cooler that you can manage by yourself.

❑ Fill your propane bottle or get another bag of charcoal for your grill.

❑ Freeze a jug or several bottles of water.

❑ Restock your car's first aid kit and food stash.

❑ Choose another action.

Extras — Pick ONE

Give me six hours to chop down a tree and I will spend the first four sharpening the axe.

Abraham Lincoln

In Hawai'i, there were two items that people stocked up on when it came time to prepare for a hurricane — rice and toilet paper. Rice may not be a necessity for you, but I'm sure toilet paper is.

This chapter isn't just about toilet paper. It's about adding more than the basic necessities to your emergency stash. This step is about the extras — the extra items you can add to an emergency kit, your Grab & Go checklist, or planning and preparation. Choose ONE to add or do today. You don't need to do them all today. Maybe next week, next month or even next year, you can add one more or do one more.

ADDITIONAL ITEMS TO ADD — PICK ONE

- ❑ Check out Appendix A — Emergency Kit Supply List and add ONE more item

- ❑ Check out Appendix B — Emergency Kit for Pets and add ONE more item.

- ❑ **Duct tape** — useful in most any situation.

- ❑ **Tarp(s)** — can be used for emergency shelter, supply cover, and even be used to carry or drag supplies and individuals.

- ❑ **Work gloves** — leather gloves are good, but I recommend the nitrile covered gardening gloves for puncture resistance and less rubbing.

- ❑ **Power strip** — this can come in handy if you are having to recharge your phone along with hundreds of others clustered around a single outlet. Rather than charging one at a time, several of you can get recharged at the same time.

❑ **Paper plates, cups and plastic utensils** — saves on water usage.

❑ **Plastic trash bags** — can come in handy as rain protection, tote bag, as well as trash collection.

ADDITIONAL PLANNING AND PREP — PICK ONE

❑ **Memorabilia** — photos, keepsakes, etc. Add specific items to your Grab & Go Checklist that are easily portable and not easily replaced.

❑ **NOAA Weather Radio** — include a battery-operated or solar/wind-up powered radio in your emergency kit. This will allow you to tune in to find out what's happening in your area during an emergency. TV is an alternative but may not always have the focus on smaller communities in time of need.

❑ Buy a **pre-paid mobile phone on a different carrier** — add it to your emergency kit. Having a cell phone on a different network may increase your chances of having service available in an emergency.

❑ **Carry a whistle** — add a whistle to your emergency kit; carry one in your purse or backpack; add one to your keyring. If you are trapped by debris, a whistle will be louder and easier to use than yelling.

❑ **Find and practice using the manual release lever on your garage door opener** — most garage doors are electronically operated, and in a power outage you'll be parking your car outside unless you know how to open it manually. Don't rely on your garage door opener to be your only way into your house. You'll need a key to get into the house or garage to manually release the lever.

❑ **Identify the Exits** — when staying at a hotel, make it a habit to identify the exits. Walk the evacuation route to familiarize yourself with which way to turn and which doors to use. Identify the exits for any building you enter. Even if you've been there before, make it a habit of identifying the exits. Whether it's fire, an active shooter, or an angry parent shutting down a frat party — make it a habit to know where the nearest exit is.

❑ **Replace your smoke alarm batteries** every year (unless they're non-replaceable 10-year lithium batteries). Replace your smoke alarms every 10 years. If your smoke alarms and carbon monoxide detectors are hard-wired, they still have a battery as a back-up for power outages. Change those too. The 2nd Sunday in March (Daylight Savings begins) is Check Your Batteries Day. And December is Holiday Safety Month. Great opportunities to replace batteries or smoke alarms. Check your fire extinguishers, too.

❑ **Take a senior safe driving course** — it may get you savings on your insurance if you're over 55 but more importantly, it will bring you up-to-date on best practices. For example, if you learned to drive before air bags, you may be placing your hands on the wheel in a way that will increase injuries.

❑ **Tire Fix in a can** — this is not something you want to use in general as you'll probably have to replace the tire and the tire pressure sensors. But if you need to evacuate in an emergency and your tire is flat, this will get you out of there.

❑ **Check your auto insurance** — Speaking of flat tires — also towing and dead batteries — check your auto insurance to see if it covers these roadside services. Check with the auto dealer or the service package you purchased with your car. Some are providing additional roadside services. And consider purchasing AAA. AAA not only has roadside services but can also provide those low-tech navigational tools called paper maps that will be helpful.

❑ **Get maps of your area** and surrounding states. If you would evacuate to a family member, then get maps that can get you all the way there. AAA has maps for free with your membership, and you can purchase road atlases that give even more details.

❑ **Hurricane clips** and other things to make your home safer. Check back on Step #17 (Shelter in Place) or go to www.fema.gov/pdf/media/factsheets/2011/avoiding_ hurricane_damage.pdf.

❑ **Spray paint & permanent markers** to mark your location, leave a message for responders that animals are present or have been evacuated, or other communication needs.

❑ **Toilet paper** — enough said.

SUMMARY

Pick ONE action to take today:

❑ Pick one of the above items to do or add to your supplies.

Possible Next Actions:

❑ Pick another one.

Resources:

• Hurricane clips: www.fema.gov/pdf/media/factsheets/ 2011/avoiding_hurricane_damage.pdf

Add Notes Here ⭜

ONE action today

❑ Choose one action to take or one item to add.

Update Your Tetanus Shot

Courage doesn't always roar. Sometimes courage is the quiet voice at the end of the day saying, "I will try again tomorrow."

mary anne radmacher

Whether you're clearing debris after a storm, gardening in your backyard, or working on a home improvement project, a tetanus shot will help you stay healthy.

Tetanus, commonly known as lockjaw, is an infection caused by bacteria, *Clostridium tetani*. Tetanus bacteria produces a toxin or poison that causes painful muscle contractions. Tetanus isn't transmitted person to person, but rather enters the body through cuts or puncture wounds caused by contaminated objects. Tetanus bacteria are commonly found in soil, dust, and manure.

A tetanus shot with a booster every 10 years is the best way to prevent a tetanus infection. The vaccination is recommended for infants, children, teens, and adults by CDC (check out www.cdc.gov/tetanus/index.html for more information).

Check with your medical insurance. Most policies cover a tetanus shot at 100%. Ask your doctor or your pharmacist for a shot. Adults are given either a Tdap (Tetanus, diphtheria, and pertussis) vaccine or a Td (Tetanus and diphtheria) vaccine.

Ten years is a long time to remember, so make a note in your calendar when you got it and set a reminder when you need the booster. If you use an electronic calendar, create an event ten or even nine years and six months out. Set weekly reminders until you get the booster. If you have a paper calendar, there's usually a year ahead page, add a note and keep transferring that note until you're in the right year.

When's your next tetanus booster due?

_____

This information should also be entered in your PIC from Step #11. There's a space to write in your last tetanus shot.

SUMMARY

Pick ONE action to take today:

❑ Get a tetanus shot or booster.

Possible Next Actions:

❑ If your tetanus booster is up-to-date, check what other vaccinations you might need. Find the recommended immunizations for adults at www.cdc.gov/vaccines/schedules/easy-to-read/adult.html.

❑ Get your annual flu shot unless your doctor suggests otherwise. The first week in December is usually National Influenza Vaccination Week, but get your flu shot earlier if you can.

Resources:

• Tetanus: www.cdc.gov/tetanus/index.html

• Immunizations: ww.cdc.gov/vaccines/schedules/easy-to-read/adult.html

Add Notes Here ↘

ONE action today

❑ Get a tetanus shot or booster.

Home Inventory

Organizing is what you do before you do something, so that when you do it, it is not all mixed up.

A.A. Milne

Taking an inventory of your home and belongings no longer has to be the time-consuming task of writing down every item you own, noting purchase dates and locations, manufacturer numbers, and costs (what it cost you to buy it and what it would cost to replace it).

You can start with a quick video on your smartphone, walking around your home pointing at what you own and talking about it off camera. A complete inventory is best, but it may take more time than you want to spend today, so for this step you will make a basic inventory

Now that I've assured you that something quick and easy is better than nothing, let's start back at the beginning.

WHY IS A HOME INVENTORY IMPORTANT?

An inventory is needed to help you begin the recovery process. In the event of an earthquake, hurricane, fire, or break-in, you will need documentation of what you've lost so that your insurance (homeowners or renters) claims can be paid and you can begin the recovery.

Insurance companies require documentation of property lost or damaged by fire, theft, flood, or other causes. During such a stressful time you don't want to have to come up with an inventory from memory. Now is the time to create an accurate inventory.

An up-to-date home inventory will help with an insurance claim. It's also key to ensuring you have the right amount of coverage.

A home inventory is important to have so that you can talk with your insurance agent to confirm you have enough coverage for what you own but not more than you need. A conversation with your agent can also help insure you're covered for the hazards you might face. As you create a record of your property, you can also evaluate and discuss with your agent whether you'll want to cover the cost of replacement or just the value.

FIRST — A BASIC VIDEO FOR THE RECORD

For a 3-bedroom house, plan on 30 minutes or less as it doesn't have to be perfect, and you're not pulling individual items out to record. The goal is to create a basic picture of what's there.

Walk through each room, looking at the walls, the ceiling, the floor, and the furniture. Pull out drawers and record what's there. Open closets and cabinets and film their contents, too. If you have jewelry, open the jewelry boxes and make sure you show the individual pieces.

The focus of this Step is to do it yourself quickly and easily. If you don't have video capability, take photos. If you don't have your own video or photo capability, ask a trusted family member or friend.

Some video and photos are better than none. Do a basic walk through now and record it with photos or video.

If you or a friend can't do it, an option is to hire a professional organizer or other professional who offers home inventory services and will provide you with a CD, DVD or a video stored in the cloud with the home inventory. With a professional organizer on your team, you can go for a full, detailed home inventory or just a quick start to your emergency preparedness.

Take photos and video of your electronics like DVRs, Wi-Fi, or video game equipment. Pull out the owner's manual to get a better look at make and model. If you can easily look at the manufacturer's number do so, but for this first video, the goal is to get it done. The next step will be to take more time to collect specific information.

If you have figurines, crystal or other items in a china hutch, take a minute (and no more than a minute) to scan the shelves. Talk about where you picked something up, what you paid for it, and what you know about it. If you have appraisals or receipts handy, pull them out and include them in your video. If they're not handy, that will be an action for another day.

Take a tour of the outside of your home as well. Another video could include your car, boat, motorcycle or anything you have an individual policy on.

Video or photo your home's exterior, your car, and other covered items.

For this video your goal is to get a start. For any collection you have, you won't go into piece-by-piece detail. Save that for another video time. But scan your possessions with your smartphone and help provide a general overview of what you have.

NEXT — A DETAILED INVENTORY

Once you've made your basic video or taken pictures, you'll need to create a home inventory. You can either make a simple written list, use a spreadsheet or word-processing software, or utilize a home inventory app. You will want to include the following:

- Brand name

- Model number

- Description

- Where and when purchased

- Cost of purchase

- Replacement value

- Serial number on electronics

- Size for artwork, area rugs, computers and tv

- Warranties or maintenance contract

If you're ready to take on a more detailed home inventory, check out the **Possible Next Actions** in the Summary section.

Keep a copy off-site.

Once you have your video, photos and other supporting documentation, you'll want to keep it safe. Get it off your phone and either onto a CD/DVD/flash drive or into a secure cloud-based storage like Dropbox, Box, or Google Drive. Make several copies if you can and keep a copy outside of the house. Keep a copy of the CD/DVD/flash drive in your safe deposit box. I'm more inclined to keep a copy in a safe deposit box than a family or friend's house because they may not keep it as secures as you would. They might forget they have a copy or what is on the flash drive. In Step #27 (Backup — Computers and Files) we'll talk about creating backups.

WHAT YOU'LL NEED TO FILE A CLAIM

- A list of items — yes, a home inventory will ultimately require a list, but a video is a great record to start with so that in the event you have to make a list, you don't have to do it from memory.

- Photos or video of your property and assets.

- Receipts for big ticket items.

- Appraisals for valuable items.

ONE action today

- ❑ Take a quick walk around and video your rooms.

- ❑ Open drawers, cabinets, and closet doors. Talk about the items on video.

- ❑ Take pictures if you don't have video capabilities.

- ❑ Take pictures of your receipts, and manuals, etc. for details.

- ❑ Upload video and photos to a secure cloud storage.

- ❑ Make a copy of your inventory and store it in a secure off-site

SUMMARY

Pick ONE action to take today:

- ❑ Take a quick walk around your house and video the rooms.

- ❑ Take a longer walk around the house, open drawers, cabinets, and closet doors and record it all on your smartphone. Talk about the items.

- ❑ Take pictures if you don't have video capabilities.

- ❑ Take pictures of your receipts, owner's manuals, evaluations, etc. to provide more details.

- ❑ Upload your inventory video and photos to a secure cloud storage.

- ❑ Make a copy (CD, DVD, flash drive or paper) of your inventory and store it in a secure off-site location.

Possible Next Actions:

- ❑ Add more information to your quick and easy inventory with video and photos showing more details.

- ❑ Review your insurance policy.

- ❑ Talk with your insurance agent to make sure you're paying for the right amount of insurance. There's no need to pay for more than you need, but you don't want to face the unwelcome realization that you didn't have the coverage you thought. It's estimated that 70% or more of the homes damaged in Texas and Louisiana from Hurricane Harvey didn't have flood insurance.[12]

- ❑ If you don't have insurance, consider it.

- ❑ Check out your insurance company's website to see if they have home inventory tools you can use, such as phone apps or checklists, such as:

- o Allstate's Digital Locker® app for iOS and Android

- o Liberty Mutual Insurance has the Home Gallery® app for iOS

- o Safeco Home Inventory app for iOS

- o State Farm has checklists you can use

❑ If you want a more detailed home inventory you can:

- o keep it simple with electronic spreadsheet software (Microsoft Excel, Apache OpenOffice Calc, LibreOffice Calc, or Google Sheets);

- o write it down on paper and add it to your PIC from Step #11 (Take Your PIC — Personal Information Center); or

- o choose a software program by looking at the reviews online. One must-have capability of any program is the option to export the information into a spreadsheet in case the software is no longer supported or you want to move it to another platform. I use HomeZada.com as the phone app makes it easy to add items. HomeZada.com has a lot more capabilities such as maintenance scheduling and renovation projects tools.

Add Notes Here ⭦

Backup —
Computers and Files

Why worry about things you can't control when you can keep yourself busy controlling the things that depend on you?

Unknown

If you lost EVERYTHING in a house fire, flood, or a cyberattack — what would you miss the most? Back it up. For some, the most important items would be the family photos (on the computer or in that box on the closet shelf) — create a backup. For others, it might be receipts, invoices, and customer lists — back it up. And most of us would feel frustrated and stressed if we weren't able to use our computers because they were being held hostage by ransomware.

BACK UP YOUR HARD COPY FILES

You may have so much paper you don't know where to start. Well, start with the category of information that is most important to you.

Your hard copy files need to be backed. Start with your important memorabilia and your key documents.

Vital Records: For some hard copies like your birth or marriage certificate or military papers, your goal may not be to have a backup but to ensure the originals are stored safely. You need to protect them from home fires, flooding, etc. and store them securely. The two most common storage options are a fire safe in your home and a safe deposit box at your bank. If you choose to purchase a fire safe, check out the manufacturer's details. Each model will have a different fire rating. Would you rather pay more for a fire endurance of 1 hour at 1700°F or is ½ hour at 1550°F good enough? Check out whether the model is waterproof, water resistant, or not rated to protect from water damage at all. Your contents may survive the fire but get damaged by the water from the firefighting efforts if it's not at least water resistant.

Go ahead and make copies of your vital records and add them to your PIC (Step #11). Though the copies may not be accepted in place of the originals, you'll at least know what records you need to replace.

Photographs and Memorabilia: Your family photos might be the most important. Electronic copies are the common way to have photo backups, and there are numerous ways to create copies. You can use your copy/scanner machine and scan one photo at a time. You can also purchase a special photo scanner, take your photos to a local store, send your photos off to be scanned, or work with a professional organizer specializing in photo organizing. I do not specialize in photo organizing, so unless my client just wants basic help, I recommend finding a photo organizer through the Association of Personal Photo Organizers (APPO, www.appo.org). There may also be old family letters and other memorabilia that you can't replace. Make copies and back them up.

> For those photos, letters, and other memorabilia that you can't replace, get copies and backups made.

Important Documents: Your PIC (Step #11) may contain either the original or copies of important documents. In Step #11 you may have decided you would stick with a hard copy PIC, an electronic copy PIC, or you decided to back up your backup and build both.

Archived Documents: I'll stop you right there. If you've worked through every step in this book and returned to complete the Possible Next Actions, then go ahead and back up your old documents if you have nothing better to do. I'm not saying backups of your old tax returns, past resumes, and paid-off loan papers are unnecessary, but your time is better spent on other things, such as taking the next step in becoming better prepared or enjoying time with family and friends.

If you use a computer, continue reading. If you don't have any electronic data, photos, or files to back up, then skip to the SUMMARY on page 146 and take ONE action today.

BACK UP YOUR COMPUTER DATA

You've probably experienced data loss from a corrupted disc or drive. You may have faced the horror of hitting the power button but your computer remained dark. You may have spent days, even weeks, working to get your data and your system back or paid someone else to do it. You may have had your data backed up to an external drive and easily retrieved the files or maybe you found they were also corrupted. You may know you need to back up your data but maybe you haven't gotten around to doing it yet or don't know where to start.

Here's the general backup strategy to follow:

3-2-1 Backup!

3 copies
2 different media
1 offsite copy

3 copies — the original plus two backups

2 different media — the two backup copies should use different devices or formats. For example:

1 offsite copy — one copy should be stored offsite

You can call it the Backup Rule of 3 or the 3-2-1 Backup Plan or call it whatever you want, but do it and safeguard your data from loss.

Let's say you use Google's office suite of Docs, Sheets, and Slides to create letters, inventory lists, or presentations. Your work is automatically saved as you type and your file is stored in the cloud ready to be accessed by you on any of your devices (original). You would need two more copies on different media to achieve the 3-2-1 Backup strategy. You could copy your files to a USB flash drive (copy 1) which you keep in your safe deposit box (stored offsite) and burn a copy to DVDs because you still have a computer with a DVD drive (copy 2). Successfully backed up data.

Another scenario could be that your files are stored locally on your computer. Even though you have your word processing program save your work every two minutes, you've gotten into the habit of hitting save routinely because you've lost your work too often when the program crashed before. You keep a copy of your photos on iCloud since you have 15 GB of free storage (copy 1 for photos). When you remember, you copy the rest of your files to Box, a cloud storage and file hosting service that offers 10 GB for free (copy 1 of remaining files that may not be up to date). Every night at 11 p.m. Carbonite, your online backup service, automatically backs up your files including your photos (copy 2 and stored offsite). Data is backed up and the 3-2-1 strategy is met but the manual process of remembering to back up is a weakness.

Yet another scenario might be paying for storage and syncing files across your computer, tablet, and phone on Dropbox. Though you can access your files when you don't have internet access, as soon as you're back online, all your files automatically sync (original). You've set a monthly reminder on your phone to copy your files onto an external hard drive to back up all your files (copy 1). You know that the 30-day version history and file recovery available with Dropbox isn't really a backup so you plan to eventually get a USB flash drive and make a copy to keep at your office (future plans but no copy 2 or offsite storage). Plans to back up your data is not a successful 3-2-1 strategy. One backup is better than no backup, but take action today and make that second backup to store offsite.

You can have physical backups like the USB flash drive, DVDs (or CDs), and external hard drives. Even other computers can store your files and act as physical backups.

Carbonite, SpiderOak, SugarSync, Crashplan, and Backblaze are common cloud backup services. You can also search reviews online to find the best option for you.

Google Drive, Box, iCloud, Dropbox, Microsoft OneDrive and other cloud storage and file hosting services may or not be a backup for your data depending on how you use them.

You may even choose to hire a local computer service to set up a backup system for you. If you do, please take the time to understand how and when your data is backed up. Know how to access the backups. If you hired someone because you just can't or won't understand "those technical things", that's okay. Require written documentation of the set up. If you don't have the system documented in writing and accessible, then you'll be paying more for the next person to figure out what's going on when you change computer experts.

Your backup plan should take into account how important your data is to you and how quickly you need it. If your electronic data is personally important, then a couple of days without it while you get a new computer and connect may be okay. But if your business or income relies on data, you need to have a backup plan that can get you up and running quickly.

How important your data is determines how much time, effort and money you should put into creating a backup.

ONE action today

- ❏ Get a safe deposit box or fire safe.

- ❏ Choose one paper category to back up or copy, and take action on it today.

- ❏ Decide how you will back up your computer and take action.

- ❏ Back up today! Schedule your next backup and

SUMMARY

Pick ONE action to take today:

- ❏ Get a safe deposit box or a fire safe for your vital and important documents.

- ❏ Choose one paper/hardcopy category to back up, and take action on it today. Whether it's scanning/copying it yourself or hiring someone else to scan it — decide and take the first step to make it happen.

- ❏ Decide how you will back up your computer and take action.

- ❏ If you've decided on manual (versus automatic) backup — back up today! Schedule your next backup and commit to doing it.

Possible Next Actions:

Additional options for developing backups for your life and activities:

- ❏ Before you back up, clean out your old files. Delete older drafts and duplicates. There are software programs and apps that can help you.

- ❏ Back up your smartphone or at least certain aspects like the contact list you've built or the photos you take.

- ❏ Though this book is focused on personal emergency preparedness, if you work or have a business, plan for how you will continue to do business if your computer goes down.

Resources:

- • Photo Organizers: www.appo.org

Add Notes Here ➘

28

Get Informed

Local, state and federal governments have set up warning systems and notification strategies, but if you're not aware of them or are not connected or don't dial in, then they're of no use.

Get and stay informed. You don't have to stay glued to the news, but learn how your community is notified and decide how you'll receive the information.

You may be familiar with the Emergency Alert System (EAS), or rather, the previous version of it — the Emergency Broadcast System, which interrupted your favorite television or radio shows to tell you they were conducting a test. The Emergency Alert System has been modernized and expanded. The alerts will still come through on your radio and your TV. It doesn't matter if you have satellite, direct broadcast, or cable television — you'll get the alerts.

You may also receive Wireless Emergency Alerts (WEAs, activated in 2013). These wireless alerts look similar to text messages, but they're intended to get your attention and will tell you what action to take for an emergency or disaster in your area. If you are in the area of an alert, you will get the *text alert* on your cell phone from state or local public safety officials, or the National Weather Service. You'll get AMBER alerts from the National Center for Missing and Exploited Children. National emergency alerts can be activated by the President of the United States. You do not have to opt in for these messages and there is no charge.

These emergency alerts are "on" by default on iPhones and Android phones. You can find the alert setting on your iPhone under the Notification tab in Settings. Scroll all the way to the bottom and you'll see Government Alerts. Android puts these alerts in different places depending on the phone. The best way to find where the alerts are located on your phone is to search the internet for "turn off android emergency alerts".

We cannot stop natural disasters but we can arm ourselves with knowledge: so many lives wouldn't have to be lost if there was enough disaster preparedness.

Petra Nemcova

There is no charge for the emergency text alerts. The alerts are on by default so you don't have to opt-in to get them.

But just because I told you to search for the alerts by using the keywords "turn off" — DON'T TURN OFF THE ALERTS. You're reading this book because you want to become better prepared for emergencies and these alerts are important. They will notify you of imminent threats to your safety, extreme weather conditions, AMBER alerts, and national emergencies.

Pay attention to these alerts and assess your situation when each and every one of them comes in. It may not apply to you, but then again it may prepare you to respond if it is an emergency.

If you dismiss a notification but want to retrieve it, look for your Notification Log on Android. Android doesn't make it easy to find, but a search for "notification log android" on the internet will show you how. For iPhone users, swipe down from the top of the screen to access your Notification Center. Because an emergency is not the time to learn where your alerts went, take a moment now to find the Notification Log or Notification Center on your phone.

Take fifteen minutes and learn more about your phone and how you can retrieve old notifications.

Radio is your best choice for information, beginning with a local station which is more likely to have information specific to your community. A battery operated or solar powered radio will allow you to continue to receive updates when the power is out and other channels such as the television or your phone are no longer accessible. A NOAA Weather Radio is a great choice. Most "emergency" radios have a NOAA Weather Radio All Hazards (NWR) setting or channel. This NWR network of radio stations broadcasts weather information, weather alerts, and non-weather emergency alerts. The radio was one option from Step #24 (Extras — Pick ONE).

Get a NOAA Weather Radio that either works on batteries or has a battery backup.

Television may also be a good choice for information, directions and notice of 'all-clear'. But unless you are in the local area of the television station (i.e. live in the metropolitan area of the station) you may not get information specific to your community in a timely manner.

Maybe you live in an area that has early warning sirens located in the community. Your actions in this step may be to find out when they are tested and confirm that you can hear them. If you can't hear them, let the emergency management agency know they're not working.

There are also notification apps available for your smartphone. FEMA's app gives you the opportunity to set up alerts for up to five locations. Get informed about what's happening where you live and where other family members are.

Though technically not an app, the National Weather Service (NWS) has a mobile website that provides weather forecasts and updated observations. You can add the site icon to your home screen and access it like you would an app. Go to mobile.weather.gov, click on the *share* button, then choose *Add to Home Screen.*

What format will you use to get more details? Will you tune in to a radio station or television? If you rely on your phone and apps, what's your backup plan? Will you have a radio that doesn't rely on being plugged in to the power grid (in case of a power outage)?

BE INFORMED ON SPECIFICS

If you have children, ask questions about the school's (or daycare's) procedures for an evacuation. Know your school's plans for sheltering in place. Find out when they will be holding their next drill and how you can be involved or at least informed. Your school may already keep you informed, but if not, take the initiative and find out.

Gather information if you or a family member requires dialysis, oncology treatment, or therapy. What's *their* plan? Discuss *what*-if situations with caregivers if you have in-home care. Ask questions and find out details.

If you work for a company (small, medium or large) what's their plan? How will they alert you? What actions do they want you to take? Where is your department's or team's meet-up location? If they haven't had a fire drill lately or the emergency procedure manual is dusty, consider getting involved and offer to be a point-of-contact.

Get the NWS mobile website "app" icon on your phone.

1. Go to mobile.weather.gov

2. Click on the *share* button

3. Choose *Add to Home Screen*

If you work for yourself, what's your plan? If you are part of an organization or group (religious, network, or social), have you talked about being prepared?

Add the information you gather to the PLAN tab of your PIC (Step #11).

TUNE IN AND FOLLOW THE ADVICE

As tropical storms build, winter weather moves in, or wild fires flare up, **turn on your radio and listen to your local officials.** Whether you're sheltering during an emergency or evacuating from a disaster, turn on your radio and listen for more information. They may direct you to evacuate or to shelter in place. If evacuation is recommended or required — *evacuate*! Evacuate sooner rather than later. Do not add to the burden of the emergency responders by forcing them to come rescue you because you didn't evacuate when local authorities announced that you should.

SUMMARY

Pick ONE action to take today:

❑ Learn how to access notifications on your cell phone.

❑ Get NOAA weather radio that uses batteries or has a battery backup.

❑ Confirm that your local sirens are working, if applicable.

❑ Get an app on your phone, such as the FEMA app or add the NWS mobile site to your home screen.

Possible Next Actions:

❑ Get involved with preparedness efforts at work, school, place of worship, or other organizations.

ONE action today

❑ Learn how to access notifications.

❑ Get a NOAA weather radio.

❑ Confirm that your local sirens are working, if applicable.

❑ Get an app

Resources:

- More on Alerts:
    - www.ready.gov/alerts
    - www.fema.gov/integrated-public-alert-warning-system
    - www.fema.gov/media-library/assets/documents/26975
    - www.nws.noaa.gov/nwr/

- Emergency Preparedness:
    - emergency.cdc.gov
    - ready.gov

- Fun ways to get informed:
    - www.cdc.gov/phpr/zombie/novel.htm
    - emergency.cdc.gov/socialmedia/zombies.asp
- Weather: mobile.weather.gov

Add Notes Here ⬂

Get Trained / Get Involved

There is always a part of my mind that is preparing for the worst, and another r part of my mind that believes if I prepare enough for it, the worst won't happen.

Kay Redfield Jamison

Get trained and get involved can be as simple as taking a CPR/AED (Cardiopulmonary Resuscitation / Automated External Defibrillator) course from your local Red Cross, or it can be as specialized as training and working with K9 search and rescue, or somewhere in between.

If you're not a medically trained professional or a first responder, consider starting your training with CPR/AED and First Aid. That's information you can use to save a life any day of the week. Check out your local American Red Cross chapter to see if they have classes scheduled. Or suggest to your company, organization, or group that they sponsor a class.

If you're not sure how to get trained and get involved, go to www.redcross.org. There's a list of training opportunities in your area. The Red Cross provides many opportunities to get involved and help your community be prepared and respond. Opportunities include blood drives, home safety campaigns, and staffing shelters for local emergencies as well as supporting disaster recovery efforts throughout the US and the world.

Another group to consider becoming involved with is your local CERT — Community Emergency Response Team. You'll receive excellent training on various emergency response scenarios and know that your community is better prepared and more resilient because of your involvement. To learn more about CERT, go to www.ready.gov/community-emergency-response-team.

What training do you want? Who provides it?

_____

_____

Check with the groups and organizations you belong to. Find out if your company has a foundation or department that is active in responding after a disaster. Your church, synagogue, or mosque may have an active emergency preparedness or disaster recovery unit. Take the training they offer. Get involved.

Want more self-paced training? Check out FEMA's Emergency Management Institute at training.fema.gov/is. FEMA offers

Independent Study courses. Some may be prerequisites for CERT or just interesting to take. Seriously, some of us do enjoy taking courses to take courses, but it can also add to your general preparedness.

You may become interested in local disaster preparedness and may decide that your free time is going to be volunteering with one of these groups. And you may just decide that you don't have the time to devote to an active role, but you want to be better prepared in general. Whatever you decide, get basic or advanced trainings that fit your needs.

ONE action today

- ☐ Take a CPR/AED course
- ☐ Take a First Aid course
- ☐ Find another resource for training and take your first course.

SUMMARY

Pick ONE action to take today:

- ☐ Take a CPR/AED course
- ☐ Take a First Aid course
- ☐ Find another resource for training and take your first course.

Possible Next Actions:

- ☐ Take more courses
- ☐ Volunteer with a disaster response or relief organization

Resources:

- Training and Volunteer Opportunities:
  - ○ American Red Cross: www.redcross.org/ux/take-a-class
  - ○ CERT: www.ready.gov/community-emergency-response-team
  - ○ VOAD: www.nvoad.org
- Training:
  - ○ CDC Education, Training, and Planning: Resources: www.cdc.gov/phpr/training.htm
  - ○ FEMA Independent Study: training.fema.gov/is

Add Notes Here ⬊

Prep for Recovery

After the hurricane has ended, the flood waters have retreated, or the embers have cooled, the emergency is over, but the recovery process is just beginning. Depending on the disaster, the physical recovery for you and your community could take weeks, months, or even years.

Though the content in this step is written as if you're in an active recovery period, use this Step to **prepare** for the *recovery* process. Add the supplies you'll need during recovery to your preparedness supplies now. Talk with your insurance agent now in order to be ready later. Read this Step now and refer back to it after a disaster.

I'll focus on five areas: Health and Safety; Returning Home; Seeking Disaster Assistance; Coping with Disaster; and Helping Others.

HEALTH AND SAFETY

I know it's an understatement to say experiencing a disaster is stressful, as is recovering from it, but maintaining your health and safety is key to your recovery. Get your sleep, stay hydrated, eat as healthy as possible, and take plenty of rest breaks as you work to clean up and restore your home and community.

Clean, safe **water** is a priority — for hydration, for cleaning, for handwashing, and for wound care. As you clear debris or work to recover personal items, wash your hands and face often to prevent infection, contamination, and the spread of germs. Refer to Step #21 (Water) and Appendix H — Safe Drinking Water for guidance on water treatment.

Food safety is important during and after a disaster. If you lost power and are wondering if the food in the refrigerator (or freezer) is safe to eat, check out Appendix J — Refrigerated

If a natural disaster strikes your community, reach out to your friends, neighbors, and complete strangers. Lend a helping hand.

Marsha Blackburn

Check out Appendix H — Safe Drinking Water

Foods and Appendix K — Frozen Foods to determine if you should discard it or if you can safely eat it. This information was adapted from the United States Department of Agriculture's (USDA's) article on *Keeping Food Safe During an Emergency.*[13]

As you clear the damage from flooding, you may find your pantry filled with canned goods contaminated by flood waters. Refer to Appendix L — Using Supplies Impacted by Flood Water.

Use **protective gear** (aka PPE — Personal Protective Equipment) as you clear and clean. Add the following to your emergency stash:

❑ Gloves

  o Puncture resistant gloves, such as leather work gloves or nitrile-coated gardening gloves, are necessary for handling debris.

  o Stock non-latex disposable gloves for handling first aid needs and cleaning contaminated items.

  o Add a pair or two of the heavy dishwashing gloves to your kit to use for cleaning. They are thicker, reusable if not punctured, and have longer cuffs to keep water out.

❑ Shoes or boots

  o Closed-toe, sturdy soled work boots or shoes that fit. You need these to protect you from puncture, dropped objects, and an uneven walking surface.

❑ Long pants

  o Protect your legs from cuts and punctures. I also suggest long sleeved shirts, but you may have to balance protection from cuts with preventing heat stress.

Good wound care is important in preventing infections from contaminated debris, flood waters, and recoverable items.

- Avoid contact. Always the easiest to say, but not necessarily the easiest to do. If you have open wounds, avoid contact with flood waters or standing water. Use protective gear (waterproof gloves and boots, etc.) and waterproof bandages.

- Apply immediate first aid to all wounds, even ones you consider minor, such as blisters, scrapes, or any break in the skin.

  o Wash your hands with soap and clean, running water, if possible. Hum the 'happy birthday song' twice.

  o Avoid touching the wound with your hands. Use disposable gloves if possible.

  o Stop the bleeding by applying direct pressure if necessary.

  o Clean the wound by gently flooding the wound with sterile saline solution, bottled water, or clean, running water.

  o Clean around the wound with soap and clean water.

  o Pat dry and apply bandage.

- Seek medical attention if:

  o The wound is an animal bite

  o The wound is a puncture by an object contaminated with soil, feces, saliva, or flood waters.

  o The wound is infected (painful, swollen, red, or draining)

RETURNING HOME

Some dangers include gas leaks, structural damage, mold and water damage, injuries during debris removal, animals, and ingestion of contaminated water or spoiled food. Your local emergency management agency, utility companies, and health department will provide guidance, direction, and safety reminders. Read the announcements handed out or posted online. Listen to your local radio station. Stay informed.

If you've evacuated, stay out of the area until officials allow residents back in. There is no reason to place yourself in danger after surviving a disaster.

Stay aware of your surroundings and look for potential hazards after a disaster.

When you are evaluating the damage to your house, start on the outside to see if anything has come down on your home such as a tree, power line or utility line. Look for cracks in the concrete or bricks that might indicate structural damage.

If you smell gas, leave and call the utility company from a safe distance. If you know how and have the right tools and feel it's safe to do so, you can turn the gas off at the main. Keep in mind that a professional will have to turn the gas back on once you've shut it off.

Contact your insurance agent. Let them know the situation and get guidance on how to proceed. Response time will depend on the extent of the disaster, so the sooner you call the sooner they'll get you on their inspection list.

Take pictures or video of your home and any damage done. But never endanger yourself. Take these picture before any debris is removed or any temporary fixes, such as putting up a tarp or plywood sheet, are made. However, you do not have to wait for a FEMA inspector before you begin debris removal or clean-up.

Once you've determined that your home is safe to enter, ensure that you are prepared for the recovery work. You'll need your tetanus shot up to date (Step #25). Be sure to wear gloves and heavy-soled shoes or boots, and long pants to protect yourself from puncture wounds.

As you remove debris, be aware of your surroundings. The debris you're trying to remove may be supporting other debris that could fall on top of you. Debris and floor damage may pose numerous trip, fall or puncture hazards.

Animals may also pose a danger. Wild animals and even abandoned pets may have sought refuge in your home. Do not attempt to catch them yourself. Stop work, leave them an escape route to leave your home and give them time to do it. If they persist in remaining, contact animal control or get appropriate assistance.

As you clean, continue to take pictures or video for insurance and FEMA assistance purposes. You do not have to hold off on debris removal or disaster clean-up (removal of carpet or sheetrock, etc.) until a FEMA inspector or an insurance adjustor assesses your property. This rumor was identified as FALSE on the FEMA rumor control webpage at www.fema.gov/disaster/updates/hurricane-maria-rumor-control. Always check FEMA.gov and your local or state governments website for clarification on rumors and current scams. More on "scams" below.

SEEKING DISASTER ASSISTANCE

During a disaster, local organizations and other Voluntary Organizations Active in Disaster (VOADs — www.nvoad.org) may respond and assist you and others in your community in evacuating and sheltering during the emergency. Those same organizations and others may also help during a disaster recovery.

You will want to contact your insurance agent or company to inform them of the damage. They may have information on additional resources available to you. If a federal major disaster declaration has been made, you may be eligible to apply for individual assistance.

Before a disaster, talk with your insurance agent about appropriate policies and coverage.

After a disaster, talk with your insurance agent about recovery and additional available resources.

The vast majority of people will be helpful, caring, and honest, but disasters will inevitably bring out a few scammers and crooks, too. Here are some things you can do to protect yourself:

- Don't give money to anyone for an inspection, disaster assistance, or help with applications. State and federal workers will not ask or accept money for help in a disaster.

Always ask for ID.

- Ask to see identification. FEMA and contracted inspectors will have a laminated photo badge. A shirt or jacket with "FEMA" is not identification.

- Don't give out personal information to anyone calling or texting you. If you completed a FEMA disaster assistance application, they have your address. They may ask for directions, but confirm that they are in fact a FEMA inspector by asking the individual to provide their company, their inspector number and your FEMA registration number. Confirm a pending inspection by calling the FEMA Helpline at 800-621-3362 or by going to www.disasterassistance.gov and choosing "Check Your Status" on the menu.

- Report suspicious activity or fraud to the National Center for Disaster Fraud Hotline, 866-720-5721, or email disaster@leo.gov

- Report instances of price gouging to your state attorney general, local officials, and local news station.

What agencies and assistance are available will depend on if the situation is declared a disaster and who declares it.

Emergency response always begins locally with police, fire, and emergency management agencies working to protect their community. If the emergency exceeds the resources of your local responders, officials will request support from nearby agencies and partner organizations (such as the American Red Cross or Community Emergency Response Team (CERT)).

If local resources are not enough, the governor of a state or territory may declare a disaster or a state of emergency. State resources then become available to assist local governments. The Governor can then request federal assistance and resources.

The U. S. President may declare an emergency or a major disaster, enabling the Federal Emergency Management Agency (FEMA) to respond. Federal assistance and programs are also made available for individual and public assistance.

COPING WITH DISASTER

Recovery takes time. The same factors that help you cope with everyday life are also important in coping with disasters and emergencies. Eating right, being active, and staying connected to your family and friends will help. Reaching out to help others will also increase your resilience.

Sleeping is important as well. Add ear plugs and a sleep mask to your emergency supply kit in case you have to stay in a community shelter or other unfamiliar location. Not only will you need sleep, so will your pet or service animal. Let your pet or service animal have plenty of uninterrupted sleep after a disaster.

Your animals will also feel the stress of the disaster. Give your animal its favorite toy and encourage it to play. This will help both you and your pet recover from the stress and trauma.

Sleep and play is good for you and your animals after a disaster.

In addition to researching the financial assistance available, take time to learn about the emotional support that the American Red Cross and other organizations may offer. It is natural to feel stressed and worried about what's next for you and your family. The support of mental health professionals may increase the speed of recovery.

For you and other family members, neighbors, and friends, be aware of possible post disaster-related stress that is affecting your emotional resilience and recovery. See Appendix M — Disaster-related Stress, for signs to watch for.

Disasters affect adults and children differently. Review Appendix M for signs of stress in adults and how you can help your kids (and pets) recover.

HELPING OTHERS

After a disaster, whether you're involved personally or not, you may want to help the survivors. There are three ways to help: donate financially, volunteer, and donate goods.

Money is often the best donation to a disaster relief organization as they can purchase what they need locally.

Donating money to recognized disaster relief organizations allows the volunteer organizations to meet the needs of those impacted by the disaster. By buying goods and services locally, the relief organizations are also helping the local businesses and community. To find a recognized disaster relief organization go to the VOAD (Volunteer Organizations Active in Disaster) website (www.nvoad.org/howtohelp).

Confirm that the organization is legitimate before you donate.

Volunteering with a recognized disaster relief organization can help survivors and make a difference in your life. Don't wait for a disaster to happen before you volunteer. You will need training BEFORE you get to work helping others. To find a recognized disaster relief organization to volunteer with go to the VOAD (Volunteer Organizations Active in Disaster) website (www.nvoad.org/howtohelp).

Don't donate clothes, toys, or other goods unless requested.

Though you may want to jump in and grab things to donate, please check with the organization before you drop off your items. Disaster relief organizations have a list of needs and anything not on the list is added work to handle and store. DO NOT donate clothes and toys unless they are specifically requested. The best donation is money as it provides the most flexibility and is easy to transport to where it's needed. Check out your local organization's list of needed items or go to the VOAD (Volunteer Organizations Active in Disaster) website (www.nvoad.org/howtohelp).

There's one more way to help — get more prepared for a disaster. Review these Steps, check your kit and gear, and encourage your neighbors, family, and friends to get prepared.

SUMMARY

Pick ONE action to take today:

- ❑ Read this Step and mark for reference

- ❑ Review any of the Appendices mentioned
    - ○ Appendix H — Safe Drinking Water
    - ○ Appendix J — Refrigerated Foods
    - ○ Appendix K — Frozen Foods
    - ○ Appendix L — Using Supplies Impacted by Flood Water
    - ○ Appendix M — Disaster-related Stress

- ❑ Purchase unscented liquid household bleach to clean undamaged canned goods after a flood. Check out Appendix L

- ❑ Add ONE more item to your emergency kit
    - ○ Work gloves
    - ○ Non-latex disposable gloves
    - ○ Non-latex gloves for dishwashing
    - ○ Sturdy shoes
    - ○ Long pants
    - ○ Ear plugs
    - ○ Sleep mask

- ❑ Call your insurance agent to talk about the recovery process in the event of a disaster. Some questions to ask are:
    - ○ when to call,
    - ○ what information they'll need,
    - ○ ask "what-if" a large-scale disaster happens and an agent isn't available to inspect in a timely

---

ONE action today

- ❑ Review Appendices

- ❑ Purchase unscented liquid bleach

Add to your kit:

- ❑ Work gloves

- ❑ Disposable gloves

- ❑ Dishwashing gloves

- ❑ Sturdy shoes

- ❑ Long pants

- ❑ Ear plugs

- ❑ Sleep mask

- ❑ Call your insurance agent

- ❑ Pre-identify where you'll donate in a

manner, can you take pictures and begin clearing debris.

❑ Identify the disaster relief organization you will donate to or volunteer with (www.nvoad.org)

Possible Next Actions:

❑ Learn how to shut off your gas safely and get the right tools to do it.

❑ Begin training to volunteer with a disaster relief organization.

❑ Take a basic first-aid course to be better prepared to help others throughout the year.

Resources:

• FEMA rumor control webpage: www.fema.gov/disaster/updates/hurricane-maria-rumor-control

• Disaster Assistance: www.nvoad.org (VOAD)

• Disaster Assistance: www.disasterassistance.gov (FEMA)

• Helping Others: www.nvoad.org/howtohelp (VOAD)

Add Notes Here ⬊

Annual Check and Refresh

Congratulations! By this step you've built your emergency kit, developed your Grab & Go checklist, and made plans for you, your family, and your pets to be better prepared for what might happen in your community. Today, this Step is to remind you that your emergency kit and supplies should be checked, rotated, and resupplied annually. Your plans should also be reviewed at least once a year. Things change — be prepared! Of course, if you've used any of the supplies you should restock as soon as possible.

When life gives you lemonade, make hot chocolate.

Unknown child

Below are several ways to keep items fresh and up-to-date. Check off which ones you'll use.

❑ Use the emergency stock as your backup supplies. You must make restocking a habit. Restock as you use items!

❑ Use your camping gear as part of your emergency supplies. Restock and add items you need after each camping trip.

❑ You can also check your kits more often. Check the contents twice a year when the clocks change.

❑ Schedule time once a year to check, review, and resupply all of your emergency preparedness supplies.

Some notable events to tie your annual review to:

o January — GO Month (Get Organized)

o March — time change

o May — start of hurricane season

o June — Pet Preparedness Month

o September — Preparedness Month

o November — time change

- o Your birthday
- o End of the year
- o New Year

❑ Set up a monthly schedule to check certain sections of your emergency kits and supplies. Here's a suggested calendar.

- o January: Reinforce Habits (fill up the car, checking for building exits, change out the batteries, check fire extinguishers)

- o February: Clothes and Personal (make sure the clothes still fit and are in good condition, wash them, replace or add personal items)

- o March: Cooking and Evacuation Gear (get ready for grilling and camping season by checking your gear and your backup cooking plan)

- o April: Financial (update PIC, rotate $, evaluate emergency funds)

- o May: Home (shelter and supplies, review insurance, update home inventory, confirm high-wind preparations)

- o June: Pets (emergency kit supplies, vaccinations, microchips, updated photos)

- o July: Food and Water (refresh and update supplies)

- o August: Grab & Go checklist (update)

- o September: Emergency Kit (replace, refill, or add supplies)

- o October: Computer and Phones (review backup plan and check emergency power supplies)

- o November: Communications and Plans (update primary contacts and evacuation plans, remind family about communication plan and meet-up locations) o   December: Health (update your medicines, get your vaccinations and flu shot, refresh First Aid training)

❑ Create your own review schedule using some noteworthy days, weeks, and months.

SPECIFIC THINGS TO CHECK

❑ Check the product date of the food in your emergency kit and supplies. Replace products that may exceed their *Best-By* date if it's less than a year away. Refer to Appendix I — Best-By Dates to learn more.

❑ Replace the batteries in your emergency kits. They may still be good, but use the old ones for everyday items and put fresh batteries in your emergency kits.

Replace your smoke detector batteries at the same time. You can also follow the Change Your Clock / Change Your Batteries motto each spring and fall.

❑ Check on over-the-counter medications in your kits. Change out the old and add any new items you need. Check out Step #7 (Build a Kit — Medications), if you have questions about tossing expired medications.

❑ Update the clothes in your emergency kit. Your kids have grown. You may have lost or gained weight.

❑ Update your checklists, plans, contacts.

ONE action today

❑ Decide **when** you'll review and update your kit, then...

SCHEDULE it!

SUMMARY

Pick ONE action to take today:

❑ Decide if you'll review and update once a year or spread it out, then — SCHEDULE it!

Add Notes Here ↘

Acknowledge and Celebrate

Congratulations, you did it! You took 31 small steps toward organizing for emergencies and disasters. Take some time to thank someone who helped you with your journey (especially yourself).

You may not be done; however, you've made a great start.

Remember — the *everyday* disasters that can disrupt our lives. Are you ready for these?

❑ Car breakdown

❑ Tree falls on your house

❑ Water heater fails and floods your basement

❑ Stuck in traffic due to a major accident

❑ Power outage in your neighborhood that affects your business or work

Congratulations!

As for me, I would like to thank **you**. *As I wrote each chapter for you, I reviewed my own preparedness. As I researched each topic more I was updating, reworking, and refreshing my own supplies, expectations, and knowledge. Thank* **you** *for being there to read, respond, and request. You've made all the difference. Thank you, Readers!*

I'd also like to thank the Hawai'i District Health Office personnel for the opportunity to get involved with

We don't even have a language for this emotion, in which the wonderful comes wrapped in the terrible, joy in the sorrow, courage in fear. We cannot welcome disaster, but we can value the responses, both practical and psychological.

Rebecca Solnit
A Paradise Built in Hell

emergency planning and preparing staff to respond and keep the Island of Hawai'i community safe.

And I'd like to thank my sister, Anne Holmberg, one of my amazing and supportive editors! Without her, commas would be unmanageable, sentences would stroll on, and key points might be hidden. It also helped that she too has experience with emergency preparedness. I guess organization and preparedness run in the family.

Shawndra

Appendix A — Emergency Kit Supply List

Emergency Kit

- ❑ **Water*** (bottled or a water filter)
- ❑ **Medicine***
- ❑ **Cash**
- ❑ **Food** * **& Can Opener**
- ❑ **First Aid Kit & Guide**
- ❑ **Radio**
- ❑ **Flashlight**
- ❑ **Batteries**
- ❑ **Whistle**
- ❑ **Multi-purpose knife/tool**
- ❑ **Mask & Gloves** (at least 60% alcohol)
- ❑ **Hand Sanitizer**
- ❑ **Toilet Paper & Facial Tissues**
- ❑ **Personal Toiletries & Needs**
- ❑ **Change of Clothing**
- ❑ **PIC** (Personal Information Center notebook)
- ❑ **Extra Glasses**
- ❑ **Pencils, Pens, Games, Books, Paper, Toys**

* **enough for 3 days**
(or more)

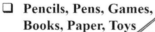

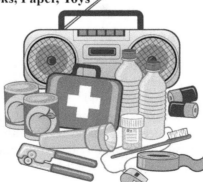

Records to put in your PIC

- ❑ **Inventory list for insurance**
- ❑ **Recent photo of each person**
- ❑ **Medical contact information**
- ❑ **Copies of bills & accounts**
- ❑ **Copies of important papers**
- ❑ **And more – see Step #11**

Your emergency kit should be portable so that if you have to evacuate, you have the basics that you need to survive for 3 days. We often leave our emergency kits at home, so think about and plan for an evacuation from your work if you are unable to return home.

To download a copy of this checklist, go to www.dhucks.com/resources-31-smallsteps-emergencies.

More details on the emergency kit items.

ABSOLUTE NECESSITIES

❑ **Water** — A couple of bottles of water and an empty container. You will need one gallon per person per day for at least 3 days but since you won't be able to store that amount in this emergency kit, you should include an empty container you can fill or a personal water filter. Refer to Step #21 (Water)

❑ **Medicine** — Make sure you have your medicine with you. Ask your doctor and insurance company if you can get an extra refill to keep in your emergency kit. Make sure that you rotate it so it doesn't get old. Refer to Step # 7 (Build an Emergency Kit — Add Medications)

❑ **Cash** — Your ATM or credit card may not work, checks may not be accepted. Collect one-dollar bills over time until you have $200. We say cash is a necessity because you can buy almost everything else. Refer to Step #1 (Save Your Ones $)

REALLY GOOD IDEAS

❑ **Food and Can Opener** — You will need to stock more food in your home kit, but include something in your emergency kit. You could add snack bars that can withstand warm temperatures. There is nothing worse than gooey chocolate pooling at the bottom of the bag. Whether you add canned food to your emergency kit or not, add a can opener. You'll be ready when you get more supplies. Refer to Step #22 (Food).

❑ **First Aid Kit and Guide** — You can purchase one or make your own. Refer to Step #5 (First Aid Kit).

❑ **Radio** — Include a battery-operated or solar/wind-up powered radio with a NOAA Weather Radio All Hazards broadcast channel. Refer to Step #24 (Extras — Pick ONE).

❑ **Flashlight** — Stick with a battery-operated flashlight or lantern for your kit. The wind-up flashlights don't last as long.

❑ **Batteries** — Add extra batteries for your items and replace them annually. You could add the new ones to your emergency kit and use the old batteries in household items, such as remote controls, where you can replace them easily and your life doesn't depend on them. Seriously, no matter what the kids say — the remote control is not a life or death issue.

❑ **Whistle** — The whistle is intended to help you call for help without going hoarse. Refer to Step #24 (Extras — Pick ONE).

❑ **Multi-purpose tool** — Add a multi-purpose knife/tool because a knife, pliers, and a screw driver usually come in handy during an emergency. Choose one that is easy to hold and use rather than the one that has numerous tools but feels clumsy in your hand.

❑ **Mask & Gloves** — Add a nuisance dust mask, a surgical mask, and nitrile or vinyl gloves for first aid needs. Add leather or nitrile-covered gardening or work gloves for working with debris.

❑ **Hand Sanitizer** — (at least 60% alcohol). Hand hygiene is especially important in protecting your health. Since you may not be able to use soap and water, pack a container of hand sanitizer and maybe even some sanitizing towelettes.

❑ **Toilet Paper and Facial Tissues** — You can never go wrong with adding toilet paper to your emergency kit.

❑ **Personal Toiletries and Needs** — Pack an emergency version of a travel kit to include tooth brush and toothpaste (many things can be handled if you have a fresh mouth in the morning), deodorant, lotion, soap, shampoo, comb/brush, contact solutions, shaver, feminine hygiene products and anything else you can think of that can fit in the kit. Travel-sized items are perfect for this.

❑ **Important papers and documents in your PIC** — Keep your important papers safe, whether it's at home or in an offsite safe deposit box. Think flood as well as fire damage. Create a quick grab file notebook of the most important papers, mortgage, insurance, accounts, etc. to add to your emergency kit. This is your PIC (Personal Information Center), Step #11. Make copies of birth and marriage certificates. Create a list of contact information for doctors, bills and accounts.

NICE TO HAVE

❑ **Change of Clothing** — Add a change of clothing and clothes to sleep in if you have room. If you don't have much room, maybe some underwear and a pair of socks. There is a feeling of civilization if you have a clean pair of your own underwear available.

❑ **Extra pair of Glasses** — When you get a new pair of glasses, keep the old pair for your emergency kit.

❑ **Pencils, Pens, Games, Books, Paper, Toys** — This is intended to keep you entertained. If you have to evacuate, you won't have your normal routine to keep you occupied. If you have kids, they will definitely need something to play with, so add games, books, cards, and paper to write on. Make these physical games and books — power or batteries not required.

Appendix B — Emergency Kit for Pets

To download a copy of this checklist, go to www.dhucks.com/
resources-31-smallsteps-emergencies.

Emergency Supply Kit for Pets

- ❏ **Water*** (bottled)
- ❏ **Food*** (canned or stored in an airtight, waterproof container)
- ❏ **Can opener** (if stocking canned food)
- ❏ **Medication**** (stored in an airtight, waterproof container)
- ❏ **First aid kit** (or add pet items to your main kit)
- ❏ **First aid book for pets**   (my choice) ⟶
- ❏ **Travel bag, carrier, or crate** (one for each pet)
- ❏ **Anti-anxiety vest or wrap** (for each pet)
- ❏ **Collar/harness and leash with tags** (cats/dogs)
- ❏ **Long leash and yard stake** (dogs)
- ❏ **Litter tray and litter** (cats)
- ❏ **Poop bags** (dogs)
- ❏ **Food & water bowls**
- ❏ **Toys**

* enough for 3 – 7 days
** enough for 2 weeks

Records to add
- ❏ **Vet records**
- ❏ **Recent photo of pet**
- ❏ **Microchip records**
- ❏ **Vet contact information**

Appendix C — Grab & Go Checklist

GRAB

Priority Items

- ❑ Emergency Cash
- ❑ PIC Notebook
  (Step #11)
- ❑ Bill paying kit
- ❑ Passports and IDs
- ❑ Safety deposit key
  or home safe

Electronics

- ❑ Phones
- ❑ Phone chargers
- ❑ Batteries
- ❑ Flashlights and
  Lanterns
- ❑ Laptops
- ❑ Laptop power
  cords
- ❑ iPads/Tablets
- ❑ iPads/Tablets
  chargers
- ❑ Portable charger
  pack
- ❑ Camera &
  charger

Medication

- ❑ Prescription
  medication
- ❑ Any written
  prescriptions
- ❑ Equipment
- ❑ Pet medication
- ❑ Cold, Flu and
  Allergy medication
- ❑ Ibuprofen/Aspirin
  /Acetaminophen
- ❑ Supplements

PREP

Priority Items

- ❑ Gas up
- ❑ ATM — more
  cash
- ❑ Buy extra
  batteries

Electronics (if time)

- ❑ Charge phones
- ❑ Charge laptops
- ❑ Charge tablets
- ❑ Charge portable
  charger pack
- ❑ Forward home
  phone to cell
  phone, if
  applicable

Medication

- ❑ Charge any
  medical equipment
  with batteries

GRAB

Clothing

- ❑ Luggage
- ❑ Jeans, 1-2
- ❑ T-shirts, 1-2
- ❑ Long-sleeved shirt
- ❑ Pajamas
- ❑ Jacket or sweater
- ❑ Underwear
- ❑ Socks
- ❑ Walking shoes
- ❑ Flip flops
- ❑ Warm boots*
- ❑ Warm jacket*
- ❑ Hat and gloves*

Comfort and Hygiene

- ❑ Pillows**
- ❑ Blankets** (or sleeping bag)
- ❑ Toothbrush and toothpaste
- ❑ Personal hygiene products
- ❑ Toilet paper
- ❑ Trash bags

Dry Goods (sweep pantry)

- ❑ Coffee/Tea/Cocoa
- ❑ Sugar
- ❑ Canned meats
- ❑ Canned fruits
- ❑ Canned vegetables
- ❑ **Can opener**
- ❑ Peanut butter
- ❑ Crackers
- ❑ Individual snacks
- ❑ Water

PREP

Clothing

* if winter

Comfort and Hygiene

** evacuation shelters may not have these

Dry Goods

- ❑ Fill water bottles

GRAB	**PREP**

Refrigerated and Frozen Foods (sweep)	**Refrigerated and Frozen Foods**

GRAB

Refrigerated and Frozen Foods (sweep)

- ❑ Cooler(s)
- ❑ Blue Ice packs
- ❑ Frozen foods easily cooked
- ❑ Fruits and vegetables
- ❑ Deli meats
- ❑ cheeses
- ❑ Refrigerated foods that are safe if unrefrigerated for 4 hours or more

PREP

Refrigerated and Frozen Foods

- ❑ Buy ice
- ❑ Put a thermometer in cooler to ensure safe temperatures are maintained***

*** refer to Appendix J (Refrigerated Foods) and Appendix K (Frozen Foods) for safe temperatures

To download a copy of this checklist, go to www.dhucks.com/resources-31-smallsteps-emergencies.

Appendix D — Digital Estate Planning

A digital estate plan is a plan for what happens to your digital assets which includes the social media accounts, email, banking apps, store rewards, and other accounts you listed in Step #12 (Your Digital Accounts — List Them) when you're gone. Your online accounts and assets are a part of your estate, but they may not be aware you have them.

Your family may need to access an account to turn off monthly payment for something you're not using anymore. You might prefer your email account to be deleted after your death.

Your spouse, children, parent or sibling may want to keep all those wonderful family photos you took and posted to your Facebook account or Flickr or stored in your Apple iCloud account. How will they access it? Will they lose these important mementos?

Have you ever had a "friend" suggestion on a social media account for someone you know has died? Do you want your profile to live on for years after you? You might, but you might also want it to be managed by your heirs.

Your online accounts are assets that need to be handled after you're gone. What do you want your heirs to do with it? A digital estate plan can be as detailed or as basic as you want it to be.

You started your digital estate plan in Step #12 (Your Digital Accounts — List Them) with the list of all your online/internet accounts. You may have made this list in paper or digital form and you are keeping it in a secure place. Adding your passwords and usernames for your accounts is the beginning of your digital estate plan.

The next step in building your digital estate plan is to check what each of your social media accounts say about what happens to your account on death or incapacity.

For example, does the sight allow you to assign a trusted individual to access and manage your account at your death.

This contact would then be able to make decisions to delete your account or download a copy of photos and posts.

Check out what each of your social media accounts says about what happens to your account if you die or are incapacitated. Each social media and digital account is different so the best way to find out what you can do to develop your digital estate plan is to search using the word 'deceased' and the account you're working on.

More and more companies now have a policy in place on how family members can close or deactivate accounts. For example:

- Facebook allows you to have your account deleted when a family member requests it and provides proof of death and relationship. You can also choose a Legacy Contact, who can then make additional decisions about the account once it is memorialized. That contact may be able to write one last message if you've allowed others to post to your timeline, update profile picture, and remove your account. I say *may* because by the time you read this, Facebook may have already changed their procedures.

- Google offers the opportunity to assign an Inactive Manager who will be notified that your accounts have been inactive for an amount of time you choose and will share any data you've chosen to share.

Your digital estate plan should include all online accounts you have (review the list in Step #12). If you include usernames and passwords — keep it secure. Let your executor know what you want done with each of your accounts, which accounts they are allowed to access using your username and password and which accounts require transfer of ownership. Include who to contact to make changes.

It's not just your retirement account that will require transfer of ownership. If you are a writer and have a published book on CreateSpace or KDP then your heir(s) are not allowed to access your account. But there is a process to transfer the account into a new account owned by them so they may continue to receive the royalties. Other assets may also require the transfer of the account to the heir(s) before the accounts can be accessed.

If there are other accounts that produce money, even if pennies a day, add them to the list and find out (and share the information) how the asset is transferred on death.

When your annual review of your will and digital estate plan is due, check up on what each of your account allows. Things change and a previous decision may no longer be the right one for you.

Possible Next Actions:

❑ Though this section was about digital estate planning, another action you can take is to draft or update your will. For help with a will, check out NOLO books, LegalShield, or contact your lawyer.

❑ Draft or update your medical power-of-attorney or living will. Most states provide a downloadable copy of the accepted format of living wills.

Appendix E — Family Communication Plan

Build your Family Communication Plan and include a copy in your PIC (Step #11), behind the first tab. This form is available for download at www.dhucks.com/resources-31-smallsteps-emergencies.

Family Communication Plan

TEXT INSTEAD

Texts are more likely to get through.
Call 911 if it's an emergency

HOUSEHOLD INFORMATION

Home Phone: _____

Name: _____
Cell: _____ Email: _____
Social Media: _____
Other Information: _____
_____

Name: _____
Cell: _____ Email: _____
Social Media: _____
Other Information: _____
_____

Name: _____
Cell: _____ Email: _____
Social Media: _____
Other Information: _____
_____

Name: _____
Cell: _____ Email: _____
Social Media: _____
Other Information: _____
_____

Pet: _____ Pet: _____ Pet: _____
Description: Description: Description:

Where Will You Meet?

In the Neighborhood: _____
Address: _____

In Town: _____
Address: _____

Out of Town: _____
Address: _____

Who's Your Contact?

Local: _____
Home: _____ / Cell: _____
Email: _____ / Social Media: _____
Out-of-Town: _____
Home: _____ / Cell: _____
Email: _____ / Social Media: _____

WORK & SCHOOL

Work: _____
Address: _____
Phone: _____
Social Media: _____
Emergency Plan/Pick-up: _____

Work: _____
Address: _____
Phone: _____
Social Media: _____
Emergency Plan/Pick-up: _____

School: _____
Address: _____
Phone: _____
Social Media: _____
Emergency Plan/Pick-up: _____

School: _____
Address: _____
Phone: _____
Social Media: _____
Emergency Plan/Pick-up: _____

More Household Information

You can also use this for family
in another household

Name: _____
Cell: _____ Email: _____
Social Media: _____
Other Information: _____

Name: _____
Cell: _____ Email: _____
Social Media: _____
Other Information: _____
_____

Name: _____
Cell: _____ Email: _____
Social Media: _____
Other Information: _____
_____

Name: _____
Cell: _____ Email: _____
Social Media: _____
Other Information: _____
_____

Pet: _____ Pet: _____ Pet: _____
Description: Description: Description:

Are You a Contact for Someone?

Name: _____
Phone: _____ / Social Media: _____
Email: _____

Other Important Numbers

Child Care: _____
Address: _____
Phone: _____
Social Media: _____
Emergency Plan/Pick-up: _____

Senior Care: _____
Address: _____
Phone: _____
Social Media: _____
Emergency Plan/Pick-up: _____

Friend: _____
Neighbor: _____
Doctor: _____
Doctor: _____
Doctor: _____
Pharmacy: _____
Dentist: _____
Vet: _____
Kennel: _____
Poison Control: 1.800.222.1222

_____ : _____
_____ : _____
_____ : _____
_____ : _____

Add your emergency Meetup (Step #14) and your Check-In contacts (Step #15) to your family's phones and carry a hardcopy. Below are business card sized templates you can use. Print on both sides; meet up card on one side, and contacts card on the other. This form is available for download at www.dhucks.com/resources-31-smallsteps-emergencies.

Where Will You Meet?

Neighborhood: _____
Address: _____

In Town: _____
Address: _____

Out of Town: _____
Address: _____

Where Will You Meet?

Neighborhood: _____
Address: _____

In Town: _____
Address: _____

Out of Town: _____
Address: _____

Where Will You Meet?

Neighborhood: _____
Address: _____

In Town: _____
Address: _____

Out of Town: _____
Address: _____

Where Will You Meet?

Neighborhood: _____
Address: _____

In Town: _____
Address: _____

Out of Town: _____
Address: _____

Where Will You Meet?

Neighborhood: _____
Address: _____

In Town: _____
Address: _____

Out of Town: _____
Address: _____

Where Will You Meet?

Neighborhood: _____
Address: _____

In Town: _____
Address: _____

Out of Town: _____
Address: _____

Where Will You Meet?

Neighborhood: _____
Address: _____

In Town: _____
Address: _____

Out of Town: _____
Address: _____

Where Will You Meet?

Neighborhood: _____
Address: _____

In Town: _____
Address: _____

Out of Town: _____
Address: _____

Where Will You Meet?

Neighborhood: _____
Address: _____

In Town: _____
Address: _____

Out of Town: _____
Address: _____

Where Will You Meet?

Neighborhood: _____
Address: _____

In Town: _____
Address: _____

Out of Town: _____
Address: _____

Who's Your Contact?

ICE / #: _____

Local: _____
Home: _____ / Cell: _____
Email: _____ / Social Media: _____

Out-of-Town: _____
Home: _____ / Cell: _____
Email: _____ / Social Media: _____

Who's Your Contact?

ICE / #: _____

Local: _____
Home: _____ / Cell: _____
Email: _____ / Social Media: _____

Out-of-Town: _____
Home: _____ / Cell: _____
Email: _____ / Social Media: _____

Who's Your Contact?

ICE / #: _____

Local: _____
Home: _____ / Cell: _____
Email: _____ / Social Media: _____

Out-of-Town: _____
Home: _____ / Cell: _____
Email: _____ / Social Media: _____

Who's Your Contact?

ICE / #: _____

Local: _____
Home: _____ / Cell: _____
Email: _____ / Social Media: _____

Out-of-Town: _____
Home: _____ / Cell: _____
Email: _____ / Social Media: _____

Who's Your Contact?

ICE / #: _____

Local: _____
Home: _____ / Cell: _____
Email: _____ / Social Media: _____

Out-of-Town: _____
Home: _____ / Cell: _____
Email: _____ / Social Media: _____

Who's Your Contact?

ICE / #: _____

Local: _____
Home: _____ / Cell: _____
Email: _____ / Social Media: _____

Out-of-Town: _____
Home: _____ / Cell: _____
Email: _____ / Social Media: _____

Who's Your Contact?

ICE / #: _____

Local: _____
Home: _____ / Cell: _____
Email: _____ / Social Media: _____

Out-of-Town: _____
Home: _____ / Cell: _____
Email: _____ / Social Media: _____

Who's Your Contact?

ICE / #: _____

Local: _____
Home: _____ / Cell: _____
Email: _____ / Social Media: _____

Out-of-Town: _____
Home: _____ / Cell: _____
Email: _____ / Social Media: _____

Who's Your Contact?

ICE / #: _____

Local: _____
Home: _____ / Cell: _____
Email: _____ / Social Media: _____

Out-of-Town: _____
Home: _____ / Cell: _____
Email: _____ / Social Media: _____

Who's Your Contact?

ICE / #: _____

Local: _____
Home: _____ / Cell: _____
Email: _____ / Social Media: _____

Out-of-Town: _____
Home: _____ / Cell: _____
Email: _____ / Social Media: _____

Appendix F — Questions to Ask

Planning and preparing for emergencies and disasters requires you to think *what if...* and then take action to prevent possible outcomes from happening or add supplies and reminders (aka checklists) to be ready when something does happen. *What if...* also allows you to plan how you might respond during an emergency and what you might need to recover from a disaster.

Basic Questions to Identify Possible Hazards

- What disaster declarations have been made in my state in the last five years? Use www.fema.gov/disasters.

- Am I in a floodplain? In an area prone to earthquakes? Near a volcano?

- Is my community prone to seasonal hazards? Hurricanes, tornadoes, winter storms?

- There have been a few disasters in the news lately. Are they likely to occur in my area? If so, what would I do to prepare?

Expand to Include Other Times and Places

- *What if* there's a tornado warning at 2 pm on Tuesday? Where will I be?
    - Where would I go if I could see the twister?
    - Where are the other members of my family?
    - What will they do?
    - How will we communicate?

- *What if* I smell a gas leak at 9 pm on a Friday? What's the first thing I should do?
    - What does a gas leak smell like?
    - Who would I call? Is that number in my mobile phone?

- *What if* the smoke alarm goes off in the middle of the night? How will I get out of the house?
  - What's another way out of the room?
  - Where will we meet up?
  - If pets sleep in the room, what will I need to control them and get them safely out with me?

- *What if* I was stuck in traffic on the way to work or grocery shopping? What supplies might I need to have with me in the winter? In the summer?

Special Considerations

- What life-saving equipment, medicine, assistive devices, or treatment do I require?
  - Does it need power?
  - Does it need refrigeration?
  - Does it need space to maneuver?
  - If I can't go for my normal treatment, what happens? What's my backup?

- If I can't evacuate myself, who will I contact for assistance? What will I need to take with me?

- Are there any special dietary considerations I need to be prepared for if I'm not at home?

Make It a Game

- Whether you have kids or not, check out the games, puzzles, and resources at:
  - www.ready.gov/kids/games
  - www.nfpa.org/Public-Education
  - www.cdc.gov/phpr/readywrigley

- Make up your own board game, write questions on index cards, and roll the dice. Or have the kids create the game and play it together on Family Game Night.

Appendix G — Sheltering in Place for Other Hazards

Radiation, chemical, biological or pandemic hazards are less likely than the natural hazards we face each year. This book is intended to help you prepare for the more common hazards, but in case you want more information on the other hazards, here are some points to consider.

Choose a room for shelter

For radiation the best location is also an interior room or basement with the fewest windows and the most shielding (walls and ground) between you and the radiation source. The three factors that protect you from radiation is distance (more is better), shielding (more is better), and time (less time of exposure, but over time radiation levels drop). Interior rooms and basement spaces increases your shielding.

For chemical hazards, the best location is still an interior room but depending on the incident, a room higher in your house might be a better choice. If the chemical vapors are heavier than air, then they will lie low to the ground.

Other amenities to consider in choosing your shelter are adjoining bathroom facilities, wired phone line capability, and cell phone, television, and radio signal.

Turn on your radio and make sure you allow local emergency text updates on your mobile phone. Local officials will provide guidance and directions. Television may also be a good choice for information, directions and notice for 'all-clear'. But unless you are in the local area of the television station (i.e. live in the metropolitan area of the station) you may not get community specific information in a timely manner. Radio and a local station should be your first choice for information.

Gather supplies

For biological, chemical or radiological gather for sealing a room (if sheltering in place is advised):

❑ Plastic sheeting, 2-4 mil thickness.

 Pre-cut to the dimension of the window/door/vent plus at least 2 inches will save time. Mark each pre-cut sheet with a permanent marker for quick identification of placement.

❑ Duct tape

❑ Towels, bedding, etc. to use as additional barriers in front of doors.

For all situations:

❑ Sanitary supplies for pets (litter and box for cats, puppy pads or newspapers for dogs, plastic bags, etc.)

❑ Sanitary supplies for people if there's no bathroom available.

   o 5-gallon bucket

   o Heavy-duty plastic trash bags (use two)

   o Cat litter

   o Snap-on toilet seat and lid made for 5-gallon buckets

   o Toilet paper or moist towelettes

   o Moist towelettes and hand-sanitizer

   o Twist ties

❑ Whistle.

 Having a whistle in your shelter, emergency kit, purse, backpack, car, and on your keychain. If you are trapped by debris, it is easier to indicate your position using your whistle than it is to yell. It saves energy and carries farther. Another option is an air horn.

Create a checklist of actions to take:

If you are sheltering in place to protect yourself from contaminated air your action checklist should include;

- ❑ High or Low? If you have the option of multiple shelters in your home, determine whether to shelter in the basement or a room in the top floor of your home based on the hazard. Some chemical hazards may be lighter than air and some may be heavier than air. When local officials provide directions and information, they'll tell you whether you should shelter in the lowest level or move to a higher level.

- ❑ Bring in outside animals if possible.

- ❑ Close and lock doors and windows. Locking provides a better seal against the contaminated air by pulling the door or window tighter.

- ❑ Turn off air handling equipment (air conditioners, fans, furnaces)

- ❑ Get emergency kit and emergency supplies, if not already present and it's not contaminated.

- ❑ If there is a possibility of radioactive contamination, prevent the contamination from entering your shelter by removing the outer layer of clothing (including shoes and accessories) before entering.

- ❑ Seal windows, doors, vents (air ducts, dryer vents, flues, etc.) with plastic sheeting and duct tape

- ❑ Listen to your radio for an all-clear announcement

- ❑ Unseal after several hours to prevent asphyxiation. You don't want to suffocate if the room is too tightly sealed for too long. Sealing your room is only a temporary action.

Other Actions to Take and Resources

Biological — www.ready.gov/Bioterrorism

❑ Install a High-Efficiency Particulate Air (HEPA) filter in your furnace return duct. The HEPA will filter out most biological agents that enter the house. Hire a professional to install the filter. If it is not sized and installed properly it will harm performance, shorten life of equipment and allow certain biological contaminants to go around the filter.

Pandemic — www.cdc.gov/nonpharmaceutical-interventions/pdf/gr-pan-flu-ind-house.pdf

❑ Stock your pantry with at least a two-week supply of food.

❑ Have any nonprescription drugs and other health supplies on hand. Don't wait to get sick to buy them. Include:

   o pain relievers,

   o stomach remedies,

   o cough and cold medicines,

   o fluids with electrolytes, and

   o vitamins.

❑ Have other items you use during an illness, including

   o hand soap,

   o facial tissues,

   o hand-sanitizer, at least 60% alcohol,

   o latex gloves, and

   o disposable facemask.

❑ Practice good personal health habits NOW

   o Stay home when you're sick.

- o Stay home at least another 24 hours after you no longer have a fever (without the use of meds).

- o Cover your coughs and sneezes with a tissue or your sleeve.

- o Wash your hands with soap and water for at least 20 seconds. Hum the 'happy birthday song' twice.

- o Clean frequently touched surfaces and objects

❑ Choose a room and a bathroom in your home that would be for the sole use of sick household members.

Appendix H — Safe Drinking Water

Treating water for microbial contamination

Here are several ways to disinfect water.

First, remove suspended particles: Before treating the water through one or more of the following techniques, allow the suspended particles to settle to the bottom and decant the clear liquid or strain the water through coffee filters, several layers of clean cloth, or paper towels.

Boiling:

1. Heat the water to a rolling boil (or roiling boil if you prefer), and continue boiling for a full minute. This will kill most microorganisms present in the water.

2. To improve the taste of the boiled water or bottled water that has been stored, mix in oxygen/air by pouring the water back and forth between two clean containers.

Boiling will not remove heavy metals or chemicals.

Chlorination: Plain household bleach — that is bleach with no added scent, cleaners or color safe ingredients — can be used to kill most microorganisms in the water. Use either the regular bleach that contains 5.25 to 6 percent sodium hypochlorite or the more common extra-strength bleach, which contains 8.25 percent sodium hypochlorite.

1. Add 6 drops or a little less than ⅛ teaspoon of 8.25% bleach per gallon of water. See table below for how many drops to use with other concentrations.

2. Stir and let stand 30 minutes. You want the water to have a slight bleach odor to it.

3. If it doesn't have a slight bleach odor, repeat and let stand for another 15 minutes.

4. If a slight odor is still not apparent, discard the water. There are more microorganisms and other contaminants in the water than the bleach can treat.

Note: sodium hypochlorite, the active ingredient in bleach, will break down into salt and water over time. The shelf-life of bleach is approximately one year if stored at room temperature. However, Clorox® recommends using bleach that is no older than four months to treat water. Other recommendations online are for six months. Shelf-life will be less at extreme cold or hot temperatures.

Buy the smallest bottle of bleach available. Then replace your bottle of bleach at least annually or when the use-by-date has passed, or if there is no smell of bleach when you measure it out (don't smell directly from the bottle). If you are unsure of the concentration of sodium hypochlorite, use 40 drops (or ½ teaspoon) of bleach.

How much bleach is needed to treat 1 gallon of water[14]:

% of sodium hypochlorite	Drops	Teaspoon (tsp)
5.25% - 6%	8 drops	a little less than ⅛ teaspoon
8.25%	6 drops	a little less than ⅛ teaspoon
unknown	40 drops	½ teaspoon

Chlorination will not remove heavy metals or chemicals.

Distillation: Distillation will remove heavy metals and most chemicals, along with any microbes present. Distillation involves boiling the water and then collecting the condensation. It requires a large canning or stock pot with a cover and a collection cup. You can rig a collection cup by turning the cover of the pot over so that the handle is inside the pot. Tie the cup to the handle so that it is hanging inside the pot, right-side up. The cup should not be in the water but above it. Boil the water for 20 minutes and collect the water that condenses in the cup. Unless you have a large stock pot or canning pot, a distillation set up is not going to be an option.

If your water comes from a private well or a cistern and has been contaminated, contact your local or state health department or agriculture extension agent for specific advice. You can also refer to CDC's guidance

- Cisterns and Other Rain Catchment Systems www.cdc.gov/healthywater/emergency/drinking/disin fection-cisterns.html

- Disinfection of Bored or Dug Wells After an Emergency www.cdc.gov/healthywater/emergency/drinking/disin fection-wells-bored.html

- Disinfection of Drilled or Driven Wells After an Emergency page at www.cdc.gov/healthywater/ emergency/drinking/disinfection-wells-drilled.html

Resource

- Emergency Water Supply www.cdc.gov/healthywater/emergency/drinking/creat ing-storing-emergency-water-supply.html

- Filters
    - www.cdc.gov/parasites/crypto/gen_info/filter s.html
    - www.rei.com/learn/expert-advice/water-treatment-backcountry.html
    - www.rei.com/learn/expert-advice/water-treatment-international.html

- Making Water Safe in an Emergency
    - www.cdc.gov/healthywater/emergency/drinki ng/making-water-safe.html
    - www.ready.gov/water

Appendix I — Best-By Dates

Your milk has a *Sell By* date. Your crackers have a *Best When Used By* date, and your over-the-counter (OTC) pain reliever has an *Expiration* date. Does this mean the store has to pull these products off the shelf? Does it mean you shouldn't drink it, eat it, or take it? Not necessarily.

Here's some background on those best-by dates so that you can make the decision.

Whether it's food or medicine, storage temperature and humidity will effect the shelf life of the product. Higher temperatures and higher humidity will generally decrease the shelf life of the product. Freezing may also negatively effect some products. Follow the recommended storage instructions.

Food Product Dating

Dates are applied to food for **best quality** identification not for safety. These dates are not required by Federal regulations, except on infant formula. Infant formula is required to have a *Use-By* date and should not be used or bought after that date. Though product dating is not required (except for infant formula), all foods must be wholesome and fit for consumption regardless of product dating.

Product dating may also include *Sell By* or *Best When Used By* dates and even *EXP* (expiration), but all these indicate when the product will be at its **best quality** or flavor. If there is no sign of spoilage, all foods (except infant formula) may be purchased and consumed after the labeled product.

These dates are "open" product dates when the manufacturer has determined the product is at is **best quality**. For meat, poultry, eggs, and dairy these dates may contain only the month and the date. For shelf-stable and frozen products a year must also be displayed.

Dates on Egg Cartons

Sell By or *EXP* dates on eggs is not a federal regulation but may be required or prohibited by the state where the eggs are sold. There will also be a "pack date" on the carton if it has the USDA grade shield. Bring your smartphone with you to convert the code to a calendar date, as the pack date is a three-digit code identifying the consecutive day of the year (1 through 365). Example: February 19 is 050.

Dates on Cans

Though the "open" (*Sell By*, *Best When Used By*, etc.) is not required on cans and only indicates the date for the **best quality,** there must be a packing code which includes a "closed" date. This date is used for tracking the product and is the date the product was canned.

Discard cans that are deeply dented, rusted, or swollen. Tomatoes and fruits that are acidic will keep their **best quality** for 12 to 18 months. Less acidic products such as meats and vegetables will keep for two to five years. Store canned foods and other shelf stable products in a cool (below 85°F), dry place.

For more information, check out The USDA FSIS page, *Shelf-Stable Food Safety*, www.fsis.usda.gov/wps/portal/fsis/topics /food-safety-education/get-answers/food-safety-fact-sheets/safe-food-handling/shelf-stable-food-safety.

Expiration Dates for Medication

Expiration dates are listed on the medicine packages by the manufacturer. The date indicates how long the product is expected to remain stable and retain its strength, quality, and purity when it's been properly stored. Instructions for proper storage will usually indicate the accepted ranges of temperature and humidity.

Expiration dates may not necessarily mean you need to toss it. Here are a few rules of thumb:

- If your life depends on it — toss expired medication.

- If it has changed color, consistency or odor — toss it regardless of expiration.

- Don't take the aspirin if it smells like vinegar. It's one medication that should always be tossed when expired, or sooner if it smells like vinegar.

- Store medication in a cool, dry environment. Your bathroom medicine cabinet is rarely a good place.

For more information on expiration dates and medicine, check out this article from the Harvard Medical School Family Health Guide, www.health.harvard.edu/staying-healthy/drug-expiration-dates-do-they-mean-anything.

Resources

- Food Product Dating (*Best-By*): www.fsis.usda.gov /wps/portal/fsis/topics/food-safety-education/get-answers/food-safety-fact-sheets/food-labeling/food-product-dating/food-product-dating

- Food Safety: www.fsis.usda.gov/wps/portal/fsis/topics /food-safety-education/get-answers/food-safety-fact-sheets/safe-food-handling/shelf-stable-food-safety

- MREs: www.thereadystore.com/food-storage/7/what-is-the-shelf-life-of-mres/

- Medicines: www.health.harvard.edu/staying-healthy/drug-expiration-dates-do-they-mean-anything

Appendix J — Refrigerated Foods: When to Keep and When to Toss

FOOD	Held above 40°F for over 2 hours
MEAT, POULTRY, SEAFOOD	
Raw or leftover cooked meat, poultry, fish, or seafood; soy meat substitutes	Discard
Thawing meat or poultry	Discard
Meat, tuna, shrimp, chicken, or egg salad	Discard
Gravy, stuffing, broth	Discard
Lunchmeats, hot dogs, bacon, sausage, dried beef	Discard
Pizza, with any topping	Discard
Canned hams labeled "Keep Refrigerated"	Discard
Canned meats and fish, opened	Discard
CHEESE	
Soft Cheeses: blue/bleu, Roquefort, Brie, Camembert, cottage, cream, Monterey Jack, ricotta, mozzarella, etc.	Discard
Hard Cheeses: Cheddar, Colby, Swiss, Parmesan, provolone, Romano	Safe to Keep
Processed Cheeses	Safe to Keep
Shredded Cheeses	Discard
Low-fat Cheeses	Discard
Grated Parmesan, Romano, or combo (in can or jar)	Safe to Keep
DAIRY	
Milk, cream, sour cream, buttermilk, evaporated milk, yogurt, eggnog, soy milk	Discard
Butter, margarine	Safe to Keep
Baby formula, opened	Discard

FOOD	Held above 40°F for over 2 hours
EGGS	
Fresh eggs, hard-cooked in shell, egg dishes, egg products	Discard
Custards and puddings	Discard
CASSEROLES, SOUPS, STEWS	Discard
FRUITS	
Fresh fruits, cut	Discard
Fruit juices, opened	Safe to Keep
Canned fruits, opened	Safe to Keep
Fresh fruits, coconut, raisins, dried fruits, candied fruits, dates	Safe to Keep
SAUCES, SPREADS, JAMS	
Opened mayonnaise, tartar sauce, horseradish	Discard if above 50°F for over 8 hrs.
Peanut butter	Safe to Keep
Jelly, relish, taco sauce, mustard, catsup, olives, pickles	Safe to Keep
Worcestershire, soy, barbecue, Hoisin sauces	Safe to Keep
Fish sauces (oyster sauce)	Discard
Opened vinegar-based dressings	Safe to Keep
Opened creamy-based dressings	Discard
Spaghetti sauce, opened jar	Discard
BREAD, CAKES, COOKIES, PASTA, GRAINS	
Bread, rolls, cakes, muffins, quick breads, tortillas	Safe to Keep
Refrigerator biscuits, rolls, cookie dough	Discard
Cooked pasta, rice, potatoes	Discard
Pasta salads with mayonnaise or vinaigrette	Discard
Fresh pasta	Discard
Cheesecake	Discard
Breakfast foods-waffles, pancakes, bagels	Safe to Keep

FOOD	Held above 40°F for over 2 hours
PIES, PASTRY	
Pastries, cream filled	Discard
Pies-custard, cheese filled, or chiffon; quiche	Discard
Pies, fruit	Safe to Keep
VEGETABLES	
Fresh mushrooms, herbs, spices	Safe to Keep
Greens, pre-cut, pre-washed, packaged	Discard
Vegetables, raw	Safe to Keep
Vegetables, cooked; tofu	Discard
Vegetable juice, opened	Discard
Baked potatoes	Discard
Commercial garlic in oil	Discard
Potato salad	Discard

Source: United States Department of Agriculture (USDA), Keeping Food Safe During an Emergency, www.fsis.usda.gov/wps/portal/fsis/topics/food-safety-education/get-answers/food-safety-fact-sheets/emergency-preparedness/keeping-food-safe-during-an-emergency. Accessed 24 Nov. 2017.

Appendix K — Frozen Foods: When to Keep and When to Toss

FOOD	Still contains ice crystals and feels as cold as if refrigerated	Thawed. Held above 40°F for over 2 hours
MEAT, POULTRY, SEAFOOD		
Beef, veal, lamb, pork, and ground meats	Refreeze	Discard
Poultry and ground poultry	Refreeze	Discard
Variety meats (liver, kidney, heart, chitterlings)	Refreeze	Discard
Casseroles, stews, soups	Refreeze	Discard
Fish, shellfish, breaded seafood products	Refreeze Some texture and flavor loss	Discard
DAIRY		
Milk	Refreeze Some texture loss	Discard
Eggs (out of shell) and egg products	Refreeze	Discard
Ice cream, frozen yogurt	Discard	Discard
Cheese (soft and semi-soft)	Refreeze Some texture loss	Discard
Hard cheeses	Refreeze	Refreeze
Shredded cheeses	Refreeze	Discard
Casseroles containing milk, cream, eggs, soft cheeses	Refreeze	Discard
Cheesecake	Refreeze	Discard
FRUITS		
Juices	Refreeze	Refreeze Discard if mold, yeasty smell, or sliminess develops
Home or commercially packaged	Refreeze Some texture and flavor change	Refreeze Discard if mold, yeasty smell, or sliminess develops

FOOD	Still contains ice crystals and feels as cold as if refrigerated	Thawed. Held above 40°F for over 2 hours
VEGETABLES		
Juices	Refreeze	Discard if held above 40°F for 6 hours.
Home or commercially packaged or blanched	Refreeze Some texture and flavor loss	Discard if held above 40°F for 6 hours.
BREADS, PASTRIES		
Breads, rolls, muffins, cakes (without custard fillings)	Refreeze	Refreeze
Cakes, pies, pastries with custard or cheese filling	Refreeze	Discard
Pie crusts, commercial and homemade bread dough	Refreeze Some quality loss	Refreeze. Considerable quality loss
OTHER		
Casseroles-pasta, rice based	Refreeze	Discard
Flour, cornmeal, nuts	Refreeze	Refreeze
Breakfast items-waffles, pancakes, bagels	Refreeze	Refreeze
Frozen meal, entree, specialty items (pizza, sausage and biscuit, meat pie, convenience foods)	Refreeze	Discard

Source: United States Department of Agriculture (USDA), Keeping Food Safe During an Emergency, www.fsis.usda.gov/wps/portal/fsis/topics/food-safety-education/get-answers/food-safety-fact-sheets/emergency-preparedness/keeping-food-safe-during-an-emergency. Accessed 24 Nov. 2017.

Appendix L — Using Supplies Impacted by Flood Water

Flood waters may be contaminated with sewage and hazardous chemicals. Any items that come in contact with flood waters should be washed and decontaminated.

Cleaning Food Package (cans and retort packages)

You may not have to toss all your food even if it has come in contact with flood waters. Canned and "retort" packaged foods may be safe once the packaging has been cleaned and sanitized.

Example of a retort package — the food packaging is made from laminates of flexible plastics and metals. Common in MREs (Meals, Ready-to-Eat), camping food, and individual servings of juices.

1. **Remove the labels** if possible. Dirt and bacteria may hide behind the label. Though the last step has you relabeling these items, you may need to mark them now in some way so you won't forget what is in each can or package.

2. **Remove any visible dirt** or mud.

3. **Wash** the cans and retort packages with soap and water. Use hot water if possible.

4. **Rinse** the packaged food with potable (safe to drink) water

5. **Sanitize** the cans and retort packages.

   • Place the packages and cans in a bleach solution. Use 1 cup of unscented, 5.25% household bleach for every 5 gallons of clean water. For the more concentrated bleach (8.25%) you can use ¾ cup per 5 gallons. Soak for at least 15 minutes.

6. **Air dry** sanitized cans and retort packages. Allow at least one hour before opening or storing.

7. **Relabel** with a permanent marking pen. Include the expiration date. If you don't re-label, you'll be enjoying a number of 'surprise' meals.

Resources

- Centers for Disease Control and Prevention (CDC), *Clean Up Safely After a Disaster:* www.cdc.gov/disasters/cleanup/facts.html

- Centers for Disease Control and Prevention (CDC), *Household Cleaning & Sanitizing:* www.cdc.gov/healthywater/emergency/cleaning-sanitizing/household-cleaning-sanitizing.html

- U.S. Food & Drug Administration (FDA), *How to Save Undamaged Food Packages Exposed to Flood Water:* www.fda.gov/food/resourcesforyou/consumers/ucmo 76881.htm#how

Appendix M — Disaster–Related Stress

Recognize Signs of Disaster-Related Stress
(www.ready.gov/coping-with-disaster)

When adults have the following signs, they might need crisis counseling or stress management assistance:

- Difficulty communicating thoughts.
- Difficulty sleeping.
- Difficulty maintaining balance in their lives.
- Low threshold of frustration.
- Increased use of drugs/alcohol.
- Limited attention span.
- Poor work performance.
- Headaches/stomach problems.
- Tunnel vision/muffled hearing.
- Colds or flu-like symptoms.
- Disorientation or confusion.
- Difficulty concentrating.
- Reluctance to leave home.
- Depression, sadness.
- Feelings of hopelessness.
- Mood-swings and easy bouts of crying.
- Overwhelming guilt and self-doubt.
- Fear of crowds, strangers, or being alone.

Helping Children Cope
(www.ready.gov/kids/parents/coping)

- Listen to your kids. Validate their concerns.

- Answer questions simply and honestly.

- Be calm and reassuring.

- Allow children to contribute to the recovery plan. Everyone needs to feel they can contribute.

- Shut off the TV. Repeated images and stories about the disaster may cause additional stress. Children may think the emergency is not over.

- Stay connected and find support for your needs within your family, friends, community organizations, and faith-based groups. If you are supported, you're available to support your kids.

- Kids at different ages will react differently and will need different kinds of support and help to recover. Go to www.ready.gov/kids/parents/coping for more information on frequently asked questions for the different ages or developmental stages.

Helping Pets Recover

- Keep your pets under direct control until you've checked fences and cleared debris or other hazards.

- Allow service animals and pets plenty of uninterrupted sleep to recover.

- Re-establish routine activities as soon as possible.

- Provide favorite or familiar toys and enjoy some play time. It's good for both of you. Or spend some quiet time petting your animal.

Resources

- American Veterinary Medical Association (AVMA), www.avma.org/public/EmergencyCare/Pages/Pets-and-Disasters.aspx

- CDC, emergency.cdc.gov/coping/index.asp

- Ready.gov: www.ready.gov/coping-with-disaster

- Ready.gov: www.ready.gov/kids/parents/coping

- Substance Abuse and Mental Health Services Administration (SAMHSA): www.samhsa.gov/disaster-preparedness

Appendix N — Car Emergency Kit

To download a copy of this checklist, go to www.dhucks.com/resources-31-smallsteps-emergencies.

Emergency Supplies for Your Car

In addition to an Emergency Kit add:

- ❑ **Jumper Cables** or better yet – a Portable Jump Starter
- ❑ **Flares or reflective triangle**
- ❑ **Car cell phone charger**
- ❑ **Flashlight**
- ❑ **Leashes** (if you travel with pets)

In WINTER add:

- ❑ **Ice scraper**
- ❑ **Warm coat**
- ❑ **Warm boots**
- ❑ **Extra gloves, hat, and scarf**
- ❑ **Blanket**
- ❑ **Cat litter or sand** for traction
- ❑ **Snow shovel**

Also

- ❑ **Fill up your gas tank at half-empty**
- ❑ **Keep tires inflated**
- ❑ **Check-up & fill fluids before trips**

Appendix O — Business Continuity Planning — Basics

You may own a business, be an employee at a company, or be self-employed. This book is not intended to cover emergency planning for businesses, however, if your business or employer is impacted by an emergency or disaster, your life and livelihood will also be affected. Here are five general areas to review and questions to ask to help your business prepare for emergencies and disasters. Go to www.ready.gov/business for more information.

INSURANCE

What coverage do you HAVE? What coverage do you NEED?

Insurance Coverage	HAVE?	NEED?
Electronic Data Recovery	☐	☐
Business Property	☐	☐
Flood or Water Damage	☐	☐
Power Outage Losses	☐	☐
Business Interruption	☐	☐
Service Interruption (utilities)	☐	☐

❑ Make an up-to-date inventory (video, photos, list)

Resources: your insurance agent and other agents in your network

DATA

Is it backed up? Use the 3-2-1 Backup Strategy

- ❑ 3 copies
- ❑ 2 different media
- ❑ 1 offsite copy

What's your PLAN B if ...?

- Your laptop/computer crashes
- There's no power

How secure is our data?

Resources: www.staysafeonline.org and your computer expert

MONEY (Income & Expenses)

What do you need to stay in business?

- Income / Customers
- Supplies / Vendors
- Products & Services / Employees

What's the PLAN B if you can't work in your "office"?

What's your vendor's PLAN B if they can't deliver?

What's your PLAN B for paying employees, vendors, and receiving payment if there's no power?

What if your website goes down?

Resources: your Profit & Loss Statement, your accountant & web designer

COMMUNICATION

How will you communicate with...?

- Employees

- Customers

- Vendors

- Community / Organizations

PEOPLE

What's your communication plan? See COMMUNICATION (above).

What's your plan for working off-site? See MONEY (above).

Are your employees, vendors, and customers prepared? How can you help them be better prepared?

For more resources and detailed business continuity planning go to www.ready.gov/business.

To download a copy of this checklist, go to www.dhucks.com/resources-31-smallsteps-emergencies.

Appendix P — Hazards & Mitigation

Resources to plan for and mitigate the following hazards

- ❏ Active Shooter — if you have children in school, does the school have an Active Shooter plan?

    - ○ www.ready.gov/active-shooter

        1. RUN and escape, if possible.

        2. HIDE, if escape is not possible

        3. FIGHT as an absolute last resort

- ❏ Bioterrorism

    - ○ www.ready.gov/Bioterrorism

- ❏ Chemical Emergencies (terrorist attack with chemical agents)

    - ○ www.ready.gov/chemical

- ❏ Cyber Security

    - ○ www.ready.gov/Cyber-Security

- ❏ Dam/Levee Failure

    - ○ See Floods, www.ready.gov/floods

- ❏ Drought

    - ○ www.ready.gov/drought

- ❏ Earthquakes

    - ○ www.ready.gov/earthquakes

        1. DROP

        2. COVER

        3. HOLD ON

- ❑ Explosions
    - ○ www.ready.gov/explosions
- ❑ Extreme Heat (heat wave)
    - ○ www.ready.gov/heat
- ❑ Floods
    - ○ www.ready.gov/floods
- ❑ Gremlins
    - ○ Don't get them wet or feed them after midnight
- ❑ Hazardous Materials Incidents — do you live near railway or a road with truck traffic?
    - ○ www.ready.gov/hazardous-materials-incidents
- ❑ House Fires
    - ○ www.ready.gov/home-fires
- ❑ Household Chemical Emergencies
    - ○ www.ready.gov/household-chemical-emergencies
- ❑ Hurricanes
    - ○ www.ready.gov/hurricanes
    - ○ www.fema.gov/pdf/media/factsheets/2011/avoiding_hurricane_damage.pdf
    - ○ www.fema.gov/residential-safe-rooms
    - ○ www.fema.gov/fema-p-320-taking-shelter-storm-building-safe-room-your-home-or-small-business
    - ○ www.nhc.noaa.gov/climo/

- o   www.nhc.noaa.gov/aboutsshws.php

❑ Landslides and Debris Flow

- o   www.ready.gov/landslides-debris-flow

❑ Nuclear Blast

- o   www.ready.gov/nuclear-blast

❑ Nuclear Power Plants

- o   www.ready.gov/nuclear-power-plants

❑ Pandemic

- o   www.cdc.gov/nonpharmaceutical-interventions/pdf/gr-pan-flu-ind-house.pdf

- o   www.ready.gov/pandemic

❑ Power Outages

- o   www.ready.gov/power-outages

❑ Radiation and Radiological Dispersion Device

- o   www.ready.gov/radiological-dispersion-device

- o   emergency.cdc.gov/radiation/index.asp
    1. GET INSIDE
    2. STAY INSIDE
    3. STAY TUNED

❑ Severe Weather

- o   www.ready.gov/severe-weather

❑ Snowstorms and Extreme Cold

- o   www.ready.gov/winter-weather

- [ ] Space Weather — solar flares and coronal mass ejections can effect the performance of technology on Earth.

  - o www.ready.gov/space-weather

- [ ] Terrorism

- [ ] Thunderstorms and Lightning

  - o www.ready.gov/thunderstorms-lightning

- [ ] Tornadoes

  - o www.ready.gov/tornadoes

  - o www.fema.gov/residential-safe-rooms

  - o www.fema.gov/fema-p-320-taking-shelter-storm-building-safe-room-your-home-or-small-business

- [ ] Tribbles

  - o DO NOT feed them

- [ ] Tsunamis

  - o www.ready.gov/tsunamis

- [ ] Volcanoes and lava flow (volcanic eruption)

  - o www.ready.gov/volcanoes

- [ ] Wildfires

  - o www.ready.gov/wildfires

- [ ] Zombies

  - o www.cdc.gov/phpr/zombie/novel.htm

  - o emergency.cdc.gov/socialmedia/zombies.asp

Notes

[1] Stephen J. Blumberg, Ph.D., and Julian V. Luke, "Wireless Substitution: Early Release of Estimates from the National Health Interview Survey, July–December 2016," *CDC/National Center for Health Statistics*, May 2017, accessed November 24, 2017. https://www.cdc.gov/nchs/data/nhis/earlyrelease/wireless201705.PDF.

[2] Maeve Duggan, "Cell Phone Activities 2013," *Pew Research Center*: *Internet & Technology*, September 19, 2013, accessed November 24, 2017. http://www.pewinternet.org/2013/09/19/cell-phone-activities-2013.

[3] Monica Anderson and Andrew Perrin "13% of Americans don't use the internet. Who are they?," *Pew Research Center*, September 7, 2016, accessed November 24, 2017. http://www.pewresearch.org/fact-tank/2016/09/07/some-americans-dont-use-the-internet-who-are-they/.

[4] If you can't quite remember the difference between a **Watch** or a **Warning,** consider two ways that help me remember. Watch has fewer letters so it come first and Warning has more letters so it comes last. The second stratagem that helps me is when I'm Watching I'm looking for something that may or not be there. A Warning means I'm likely to find it soon. For a more precise and scientific explanation go to http://www.weather.gov/lwx/WarningsDefined. Accessed January 28, 2018.

[5] "Hurricane Katrina," *Louisiana SPCA*, accessed January 28, 2018. https://www.la-spca.org/katrina.

[6] Robert Meyerand and Howard Kunreuther, *The Ostrich Paradox: Why We Underprepare for Disasters*, Kindle Edition, Loc 632.

[7] "Hurricane Katrina," *Louisiana SPCA*, accessed January 28, 2018. https://www.la-spca.org/katrina.

[8] R. J. Maughan and J. Griffin, "Caffeine ingestion and fluid balance: a review*," Journal of Human Nutrition and Dietetics*, 2003 Dec; 16(6): 411 – 420.

[9] Oren Dorell, "By the numbers: More than half of Puerto Rico still without drinking water," *USA Today*, September 30, 2017, accessed December 19, 2017. https://www.usatoday.com/story/news/nation/2017/09/30/puerto-rico-by-the-numbers/720731001/.

[10] The Associate Press, "Restoring power to Hurricane Sandy victims takes days to weeks; 'it's hard, grueling work'," *PENN Live*, updated November 16, 2012, accessed December 19, 2017. http://www.pennlive.com/midstate/index.ssf/2012/11/restoring_power_to_hurricane_s.html.

[11] Timothy Hurley, "State officials now recommend your disaster supply kit last for at least 14 days," *Honolulu Star Advertiser*, June 27, 2017, accessed January 28, 2018. http://www.staradvertiser.com/2017/06/27/hawaii-news/disaster-supply-kit-should-last-for-at-least-14-days/.

[12] Leslie Scism and Nicole Friedman, "Houston Residents Return Home to Scary Reality: No Insurance Coverage," *Wall Street Journal*, updated September 1, 2017, accessed January 28, 2018.https://www.wsj.com/articles/houston-residents-return-home-to-scary-reality-no-insurance-coverage-1504300222.

[13] "Keeping Food Safe During an Emergency," *United States Department of Agriculture (USDA)*, last modified July 30, 2013, accessed January 28, 2018. https://www.fsis.usda.gov/wps/portal/fsis/topics/food-safety-education/get-answers/food-safety-fact-sheets/emergency-preparedness/keeping-food-safe-during-an-emergency.

[14] "Making Water Safe in an Emergency," *Centers for Disease Control and Prevention (CDC)*, updated September 21, 2017, accessed January 28, 2018. https://www.cdc.gov/healthywater/emergency/drinking/making-water-safe.html.

Glossary

Term	Definition
AED	Automated External Defibrillator
CDC	Centers for Disease Control and Prevention
CERT	Community Emergency Response Team
Chunk of Time	A small period of time in which you work. This time period is small enough to keep you willing to organize, but large enough to make progress. It's intended to break up a larger block of time and help you refocus on your original goal or intention. 15 minutes is a natural chunk of time, but 20, 23, and 30 minutes are also common. However, 5, 7, and 10 minutes can also be used if that's all the time you have.
CPO-CD®	Certified Professional Organizer in Chronic Disorganization. Certified from the Institute for Challenging Disorganization. The CPO-CD® certified individual is a professional organizer who has been educated in depth on the issues of chronic disorganization.
CPR	Cardiopulmonary Resuscitation
Disaster	A situation that overwhelms available resources.
Disinfect	Destruction or removal of illness causing germs (bacteria and viruses). Methods include heat, chemicals, ultraviolet (UV) light, and solar radiation. Filtration may remove bacteria but not viruses from the water if the filter size is between 0.1 and 0.4 microns. Reverse osmosis and newer filtration technology may remove viruses.
Emergency	A situation that calls for immediate action or assistance.

Term	Definition
FEMA	Federal Emergency Management Agency, part of the U.S. Department of Homeland Security (DHS)
Filter (water)	Physically remove illness causing germs (protozoa, cysts, bacteria, and viruses) and particles. The size of the filter pores determines which germs and particles are removed. See *germs* for more details.
Flood Watch	**Be Aware.** Conditions are right for flooding to occur in your area.
Flood Warning	**Take Action!** Flooding is either happening or will happen shortly.
Grab & Go Checklist	A checklist of priority items to take with you when you evacuate that cannot be left in your emergency kit.
Hazard Mitigation	Removing or reducing a potential vulnerability in your home and workplace.
HEPA Filter	High-Efficiency Particulate Air filter
Hurricanes	A hurricane is a tropical cyclone, which is a rotating, organized system of clouds and thunderstorms that originates over tropical or subtropical waters and has a closed low-level circulation. Tropical cyclones rotate counterclockwise in the Northern Hemisphere. They are classified as follows: **Tropical Depression:** A tropical cyclone with maximum sustained winds of 38 mph (33 knots) or less. **Tropical Storm:** A tropical cyclone with maximum sustained winds of 39 to 73 mph (34 to 63 knots).

Term	**Definition**
Hurricanes continued	**Hurricane:** A tropical cyclone with maximum sustained winds of 74 mph (64 knots) or higher. In the western North Pacific, hurricanes are called typhoons; similar storms in the Indian Ocean and South Pacific Ocean are called cyclones.

Major Hurricane: A tropical cyclone with maximum sustained winds of 111 mph (96 knots) or higher, corresponding to a Category 3, 4 or 5 on the Saffir-Simpson Hurricane Wind Scale.

Category 1	74-95 mph
Category 2	96-110 mph
Category 3	111-129 mph
Category 4	130-156 mph
Category 5	157+ mph

Saffir-Simpson Hurricane Wind Scale is a 1 to 5 rating based on a hurricane's sustained wind speed.

Term	**Definition**
IATA	International Air Transportation Association
Mass Care Shelter	Shelter and services provided to a large number of people displaced by an emergency or disaster. It may be a temporary place to shelter during the hazard, such as a tornado. It may be open for a longer time period and provide food, bedding, and other care.
OTC	Over-the-counter medicines such as aspirin, cough medicine, etc.
Personal Information Center (PIC)	A physical notebook or a digital file containing essential personal information and important records such as copies of utility bills, bank and credit card statements, medical history, wills, birth certificates, death certificates and other vital documents.

Term	Definition
PIC	Personal Information Center
Retort package	Food packaging made from laminates of flexible plastics and metals. Common in MREs (Meals, Ready-to-Eat), camping food, and individual servings of juices.

Image By Bahamut0013 (Own work) [CC BY 3.0 (http://creativecommons.org/licenses/by/3.0)], via Wikimedia Commons

Term	Definition
Rx	Prescription, medicine prescribed by a physician.
Safe Room	A hardened structure specifically designed to meet Federal Emergency Management Agency (FEMA) criteria and provide near-absolute protection in extreme weather events, including tornadoes and hurricanes.
Shelter	Protection from the weather or other hazards. The best shelter option depends on the hazard. You may need to shelter for a few hours or for days and weeks. You may need to stay put and shelter in place, whether it's at home, work, school, out in your community, or traveling. You may need to evacuate and seek shelter with family, friends, or a hotel outside of the affected area. You may need to go to a community or mass care shelter with other residents affected by emergency or disaster.

Term	**Definition**

Shelter in Place — Staying put and sheltering from the hazards where you are. You may need to shelter in place at home, work, school, or out in the community. You may be traveling or visiting and need to shelter in place.

Someday — A period of time that never arrives.

Timer — An essential tool for refocusing on what you intended to do, rather than what drew your attention away. Basic requirements are an auditory or vibrational indication at the end of your chunk of time to remind you, "Hey! Get back to what you said you wanted to do right now! "

Trimline corded phone

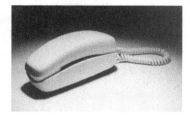

Photo by Donald Genaro (Own work) [CC BY-SA 3.0 (https://creativecommons. org/licenses/by-sa/3.0)], via Wikimedia Commons

also known as slimline or princess phone.

VOAD — Voluntary Organizations Active in Disaster (www.nvoad.org)

VoIP phone — Voice over Internet Protocol phone

Warning (weather) — **Reminder that a Watch is "lower" than a Warning**

A **warning** means that a weather emergency is already happening, or will happen soon. When you hear a warning, take immediate action.

Term	**Definition**
Warning (weather) continued	**Extreme Wind Warning:** Extreme sustained winds of a major hurricane (115 mph or greater), usually associated with the eyewall, are expected to begin within an hour. Take immediate shelter in the interior portion of a well-built structure.

Flash Flood Warning: Issued when a flash flood has been reported or is imminent.

Flood Warning: Issued as an advance notice that a flood is imminent or is in progress at a certain location or in a certain river basin.

Hurricane Warning: Hurricane conditions (sustained winds of 74 mph or greater) are expected somewhere within the specified area. NOAA National Hurricane Center (NHC) issues a hurricane warning 36 hours in advance of tropical storm-force winds to give you time to complete your preparations. All preparations should be complete. **Evacuate immediately if told to do so.**

Severe Thunderstorm Warning: Indicates that severe thunderstorms have been sighted in your area.

Storm Surge Warning: There is a danger of life-threatening inundation from rising water moving inland from the shoreline somewhere within the specified area, generally within 36 hours. If you are under a storm surge warning, check for evacuation orders from your local officials.

Tornado Warning: A tornado has been sighted or radar indicates. Shelter immediately.

Taken from www.ready.gov/tornadoes

Tropical Storm Warning: Tropical storm conditions (sustained winds of 39 to 73 mph) are expected within your area within 36 hours.

Term	Definition

Warning (weather) continued

Sources:

- www.cdc.gov/phpr/areyouprepared/informed.htm
- www.nws.noaa.gov/om/hurricane/ww.html
- www.ready.gov/tornadoes

Watch (weather)

Remember a Warning is more "serious/imminent" than a Watch

A **watch** means that there is a high possibility that a weather emergency will occur. When a severe storm watch is issued for your area, continue to listen to the radio or television for updates and pay attention to visible weather changes around you.

Flash Flood Watch: Issued when flash flooding is possible within the designated watch area.

Hurricane Watch: Hurricane conditions (sustained winds of 74 mph or greater) are possible within your area. Because it may not be safe to prepare for a hurricane once winds reach tropical storm force, The NHC issues hurricane watches 48 hours before it anticipates tropical storm-force winds.

Severe Thunderstorm Watch: Indicates that conditions are right for:

- Lightning or damaging winds greater than 58 mph,
- Hail that could reach a diameter of 0.75 inches, and
- Heavy rain.

Term	**Definition**
Watch (weather) continued	**Storm Surge Watch:** There is a possibility of life-threatening inundation from rising water moving inland from the shoreline somewhere within the specified area, generally within 48 hours. If you are under a storm surge watch, check for evacuation orders from your local officials.
	Tornado Watch: Tornadoes are possible. Move near enough to a shelter or sturdy building that you can reach it quickly if you see a tornado or the Watch becomes a Warning. Watch the sky and stay tuned to weather alerts.
	Tropical Storm Watch: Tropical storm conditions (sustained winds of 39 to 73 mph) are possible within the specified area within 48 hours.
	Evacuate if told to do so.
	Sources: <ul><li>www.cdc.gov/phpr/areyouprepared/informed.htm</li><li>www.nws.noaa.gov/om/hurricane/ww.html</li><li>www.ready.gov/tornadoes</li></ul>
Wireline phone	Standard landline phone that is wired and not VoIP (Voice Over Internet Protocol) or wireless cellular phone service.

Resources

Links to all the resource are available at www.dhucks.com/resourcelist-31smallsteps-emergency.

- 1Password, 1password.com [password manager]
- 911PetChip™, 911petchip.com [microchip manufacturer]
- 911PetChip™, www.FreePetChipRegistry.com [registration]
- American Animal Hospital Association (AAHA), www.petmicrochiplookup.org [Universal Pet Microchip Lookup Tool]
- American Red Cross, www.redcross.org/about-us/our-work/training-education [First Aid and CPR training]
- American Red Cross: www.redcross.org/ux/take-a-class [training and volunteer opportunities]
- American Society for the Prevention of Cruelty to Animals (ASPCA), www.aspca.org/pet-care/general-pet-care/disaster-preparedness [preparedness for birds, reptiles, horses, and small animals]
- American Veterinary Medical Association (AVMA): www.avma.org/public/EmergencyCare/Pages/Pets-and-Disasters.aspx [pets and disasters]
- Association of Personal Photo Organizers (APPO): www.appo.org [help with photos]
- Avid™, avidid.com [microchip manufacturer]
- Avid™, avidid.com/pettrac/enrollment [registration]

Centers for Disease Control and Prevention (CDC)

- www.cdc.gov/disasters/cleanup/facts.html [*Clean Up Safely After a Disaster*]
- emergency.cdc.gov/coping/index.asp [coping]

Centers for Disease Control and Prevention (CDC) cont.

- www.cdc.gov/parasites/crypto/gen_info/filters.html [filters]

- www.cdc.gov/phpr/zombie/novel.htm [fun ways to get informed]

- emergency.cdc.gov/socialmedia/zombies.asp [fun ways to get informed]

- emergency.cdc.gov [general emergency preparedness]

- www.cdc.gov/nonpharmaceutical-interventions/pdf/gr-pan-flu-ind-house.pdf [*Get Your Household Ready for Pandemic Flu*]

- www.cdc.gov/healthywater/emergency/cleaning-sanitizing/household-cleaning-sanitizing.html [*Household Cleaning & Sanitizing*]

- www.cdc.gov/vaccines/schedules/easy-to-read/adult.html [immunizations]

- www.cdc.gov/tetanus/index.html [tetanus]

- www.cdc.gov/phpr/training.htm [training]

- www.cdc.gov/healthywater/emergency/drinking/creating-storing-emergency-water-supply.html [water]

- www.cdc.gov/healthywater/emergency/drinking/making-water-safe.html [water]

- www.cdc.gov/healthywater/emergency/drinking/disinfection-cisterns.html [water — cisterns or rain catchment]

- www.cdc.gov/healthywater/emergency/drinking/disinfection-wells-bored.html [water — bored or dug wells]

- www.cdc.gov/healthywater/emergency/drinking/disinfection-wells-drilled.html [water — drilled or driven wells]

- Department of Homeland Security (DHS), www.dhs.gov/wireless-priority-service-wps [who gets priority access]

**Department of Homeland Security
(Ready campaign)**

- www.ready.gov/alerts [alerts]

- www.ready.gov/bioterrorism [bioterrorism]

- www.ready.gov/business [business continuity planning]

- www.ready.gov/coping-with-disaster [*Coping with Disaster*]

- ready.gov [general emergency preparedness]

- www.ready.gov/kids/parents/coping [*Helping Children Cope*]

- www.ready.gov/individuals-access-functional-needs [*Individuals with Disabilities*]

- www.ready.gov/tornadoes [tornadoes]

- www.ready.gov/community-emergency-response-team [training and volunteer opportunities — CERT]

- www.ready.gov/water [water]

- Drug Enforcement Administration (DEA), takebackday.dea.gov [local drug take back locations]

- Dhucks, www.dhucks.com/resources-31-smallsteps-emergencies [download various resources]

- Environmental Protection Agency (EPA), www.epa.gov/sites/production/files/2015-06/documents/how-to-dispose-medicines.pdf [disposal]

- Facebook, www.facebook.com/about/safetycheck [safety check]

Federal Emergency Management Agency (FEMA)

- www.fema.gov/integrated-public-alert-warning-system [alerts]

- www.fema.gov/media-library/assets/documents/26975 [alerts]

- www.fema.gov/media-library-data/1390856235302-ff6e316df62851d5a5afe834b4fcd53c/Commuter_Emergency_Plan_v7_508.pdf [commuter emergency plan]

- www.disasterassistance.gov [disaster assistance]

- www.fema.gov/disasters [disaster search by State/Territory]

- www.fema.gov/media-library-data/1420417719892-b9b41636569f3c41eea88e70ddfae2e2/FEMA528.pdf [*Earthquake Home Hazard Hunt*]

- www.fema.gov/media-library/assets/documents/6015 [earthquakes]

- www.fema.gov/media-library/assets/documents/109669 [flooding]

- www.fema.gov/pdf/media/factsheets/2011/avoiding_hurricane_damage.pdf [hurricanes and hurricane clips]

- www.fema.gov/disaster/updates/hurricane-maria-rumor-control [rumor control]

- www.fema.gov/safe-rooms [safe room]

- www.fema.gov/residential-safe-rooms [safe room]

- www.fema.gov/fema-p-320-taking-shelter-storm-building-safe-room-your-home-or-small-business [safe room]

- training.fema.gov/is [training]

- Harvard Health Publishing, Harvard Medical School, www.health.harvard.edu/staying-healthy/drug-expiration-dates-do-they-mean-anything [expiration dates]

- Institute for Challenging Disorganization, challengingdisorganization.org [professional organizers trained to help clients with chronic disorganization]

- International Air Transport Association (IATA), www.iata.org/whatwedo/cargo/live-animals/pets /Pages/index.aspx [guidance for dimensions of container]

- LastPass, www.lastpass.com [password manager]

- Microchip ID Solutions Inc., microchipidsolutions.com [microchip manufacturer and registration]

- National Association of Productivity and Organizing Professionals (NAPO), www.napo.net [help with preparedness]

- NAPO Virtual Chapter, www.virtualorganizers.com [professional organizers who work with you off-site or virtually]

- National Oceanic and Atmospheric Administration (NOAA), National Weather Service, www.nws.noaa.gov/nwr [alerts]

- National Weather Service (NWS), mobile.weather.gov [weather forecasts and updates]

- OutdoorGearlLab, www.outdoorgearlab.com/topics /camping-and-hiking/best-cooler/buying-advice [coolers]

- Poison Control Center, www.PoisonHelp.org

- The Ready Store, www.thereadystore.com/food-storage/7/what-is-the-shelf-life-of-mres [MREs]

- Recreational Equipment, Inc. (REI), www.rei.com/learn /expert-advice/water-treatment-backcountry.html [filters]

- Recreational Equipment, Inc. (REI), www.rei.com/learn /expert-advice/water-treatment-international.html

- Shake Out™, www.shakeout.org [earthquake]

- Stay Safe Online, National Cyber Security Alliance (NCSA), staysafeonline.org/stay-safe-online/securing-key-accounts-devices/passwords-securing-accounts [how to stay secure and safe online]

- Substance Abuse and Mental Health Services Administration (SAMHSA), www.samhsa.gov/disaster-preparedness [behavioral health resources]

United States Department of Agriculture (USDA), Food Safety and Inspection Service

- www.fsis.usda.gov/wps/portal/fsis/topics/food-safety-education/get-answers/food-safety-fact-sheets/food-labeling/food-product-dating/food-product-dating [product dating (*Best-By*)]

- www.fsis.usda.gov/wps/portal/fsis/topics/food-safety-education/get-answers/food-safety-fact-sheets/safe-food-handling/shelf-stable-food-safety [food safety]

- www.fsis.usda.gov/wps/portal/fsis/topics/food-safety-education/get-answers/food-safety-fact-sheet/emergency-preparedness/keeping-food-safe-during-an-emergency [food safety during an emergency]

U.S. Food & Drug Administration (FDA)

- www.fda.gov/ForConsumers/ConsumerUpdates/ucm1016 53.htm [disposal of unused medicines]

- www.fda.gov/food/resourcesforyou/consumers/ucm076881. htm#how [*How to Save Undamaged Food Packages Exposed to Flood Water*]

Volunteer Organizations Active in Disasters (VOAD)

- www.nvoad.org [disaster assistance and volunteer opportunities]

- www.nvoad.org/howtohelp [helping others]

- YouTube, youtu.be/h8CwNyfaU3g [emergency muzzle]

Resources located on the Dhucks.com website

- Download resources and links mentioned in this book,
  www.dhucks.com/resources-31-smallsteps-emergencies

- Blog, www.dhucks.com/blog

Additional Dhucks' resources

- Facebook: www.facebook.com/DHUCKSinaRow

- Pinterest: www.pinterest.com/shawndraholmber

Images

Page	Photo	Attribution
14	Fuel gauge	Photo purchased at bigstockphoto.com
19	Trimline corded phone	Photo by Donald Genaro (Own work) [CC BY-SA 3.0 (https://creativecommons.org/licenses/by-sa/3.0)], via Wikimedia Commons
35	Take Back Day poster	Image from https://www.dea.gov/take-back/takeback-day_2017_oct.html
204	Retort bag	Image By Bahamut0013 (Own work) [CC BY 3.0 (http://creativecommons.org/licenses/by/3.0)], via Wikimedia Commons

Keyword Index

so, who's this shawndra person, anyway?

Shawndra Holmberg has been organizing longer than the eleven years she's been running her business, **Dhucks**. She believes in the power that an organized space, schedule, and life have on our creative spirit. She knows there's not one right way to get organized, and she's trained to make your organization work for you. She is a Certified Professional Organizer in Chronic Disorganization (CPO-CD®) and is focused on being your personal trainer for productivity, a mentor for your goals, and a motivational force for your creativity.

On her journey to becoming an organizer, Shawndra tackled jobs as varied as bioterrorism preparedness planner for the Hawai'i State Department of Health on the Big Island, coordinated environmental and safety training on Johnston Atoll (approximately 850 miles southwest of Hawai'i), and handled health and safety issues for a year at the South Pole station, Antarctica, with temperatures ranging from a balmy -7°F to a chilling -112°F.

Shawndra considers herself a lousy tourist as she usually spends her vacations enjoying a good book (reading one or writing one) and drinking coffee on her lanai, deck, porch, or sunroom. That's why she prefers to live and work in interesting locales. She spent a year at the South Pole, Antarctica, attended graduate school in big sky country (Bozeman, Montana), worked on Johnston Island, and then thawed out in Hawai'i. She is currently enjoying the people and scenery of Western Pennsylvania as she organizes and coaches writers and others who are reaching for their dream. She is located in Pennsylvania but works virtually everywhere.

If you would like an email when Shawndra's next book is released, sign up www.dhucks.com/newreleases. Your email address will never be shared and you can unsubscribe at any time.

If you enjoyed this book, please consider leaving a review on Amazon or Goodreads. A line or two or just the stars rating would make all the difference in helping others find this resource so they can prepare for emergencies and disasters too.

and what's this about a dhuck?

Dhucks are fun, playful and cute. What better mascot for organizing or *getting your dhucks in a row*. Shawndra has had a life-long interest in getting her dhucks in a row, whether it's getting organized, losing weight, reaching for a dream, or finding the joy in each day. Join the fun and *get your dhucks in a row*.

CPSIA information can be obtained
at www.ICGtesting.com
Printed in the USA
LVHW05s2347310718
585568LV00008B/73/P